Four Catholic Pioneers in Missouri:
Lamarque, Kenrick, Fox, and Hogan

Four Catholic Pioneers in **Missouri**: Lamarque, Kenrick, **Fox,** and **Hogan**

Irish Missionaries and
Their Supporter

Mark G. Boyer

WIPF & STOCK · Eugene, Oregon

FOUR CATHOLIC PIONEERS IN MISSOURI: LAMARQUE,
KENRICK, FOX, AND HOGAN
Irish Missionaries and Their Supporter

Wipf & Stock
An Imprint of Wipf and Stock Publishers
199 W. 8th Ave., Suite 3
Eugene, OR 97401

www.wipfandstock.com

PAPERBACK ISBN: 978-1-6667-6214-3
HARDCOVER ISBN: 978-1-6667-6215-0
EBOOK ISBN: 978-1-6667-6216-7

11/08/22

Dedicated to

Marie-Louise Lamarque,
Peter Richard Kenrick,
James Fox,
and John Joseph Hogan,

pioneers all.

"Central inland race are we, from Missouri, with the continental blood intervein'd,

All the hands of comrades clasping, all the Southern, all the Northern,

Pioneers! O pioneers!"

—"Pioneers! O Pioneers!" in *Leaves of Grass*
    by Walt Whitman

Contents

Acknowledgements

N O BOOK COMES INTO existence without the help—direct or indirect—of others. This volume is not an exception to that statement. Research help was given generously by Rena Schergen, Archivist for the Archdiocese of St. Louis. The idea for this book was a seed planted by Miss Natalie Villmer, RPWCK. She, a Rural Parish Worker of Christ the King, Fertile, Missouri, recommended to me the Paytons' book on the Irish Wilderness and both of Hogan's books recently republished in one volume and edited by Crystal Payton. While I owe all of them a hearty Thank You in gratitude for their help, any mistakes in what follows are mine.

Mark G. Boyer

July 26, 2022
Feast of Sts. Joachim and Anne

Introduction

T HIS IS A BOOK about four Roman Catholic pioneers—explorers and developers—whose lives crossed each other's paths in Old Mines, Missouri, in the middle of the 1800s. Two of them were priests, and one of them was a bishop, then an archbishop. One was a laywoman, who was very generous with her riches. Three of them were not only of Irish descent, but came from Ireland. The laywoman was French, and she came from Ste. Genevieve. The Great Potato Famine in Ireland in the 1840s brought all of them together in the oldest village in the State of Missouri: Old Mines. The potato famine brought many Irish to Missouri in the nineteenth century to farm, to build railroads, and to construct churches for worship. This is the story of pioneers Marie-Louise (Bolduc) Lamarque, Peter Richard Kenrick, James Fox, and John Joseph Hogan. Their lives crossed each other's path in Old Mines, Missouri, a lead-mining village about sixty miles south of St. Louis (before St. Louis existed) and about forty miles east of Ste. Genevieve (before Ste. Genevieve existed). Old Mines was founded in 1723 by Philippe Francois Renault, the son of Philippe Renault, a wealthy iron founder at Cousolre, France. Philippe the younger was a French politician, businessman, explorer, metallurgist, forge-master, entrepreneur, and favorite courtier of King Louis XV of France. He left Picardy, France, in 1718 for the Illinois Country and Louisiana and arrived in Illinois in 1719. He came to mine lead. Because he had political connections in his mother country, he was granted land on the Illinois side of the Mississippi River. His land grant on the Missouri side of the Mississippi River on June 14, 1723, entitled him to mine lead, which he did until 1742, when he returned to France. Some of his miners stayed in Old Mines, mining, trapping, fur trading, and homesteading. Seeking entrepreneurial opportunities, pioneer Marie-Louise (Bolduc) Lamarque came from Ste. Genevieve to live in Old Mines between 1815 and 1816 after marrying Etienne Lamarque in Ste. Genevieve. The Lamarques, who were Roman Catholic, came to Old Mines to engage in lead mining and to buy and sell real estate.

In 1833, Peter Richard Kenrick, a Roman Catholic priest, emigrated from Dublin, Ireland, to Philadelphia, Pennsylvania, at the invitation of his brother, Francis Patrick Kenrick, the coadjutor bishop of Philadelphia. In 1841, Peter moved to St. Louis, after being named coadjutor bishop of St. Louis. A coadjutor bishop is one who had the right to become the next bishop after the then-current one died or was moved to another diocese, which is exactly what Peter did in St. Louis in 1843 with the death of his predecessor, Joseph Rosati. Then, in 1847, Peter was named the first archbishop of St. Louis. Kenrick was a Catholic pioneer in a huge area carved out of the Louisiana Purchase.

The Irish had been coming to the eastern United States and settling there long before 1840. However, the Great Potato Famine in the 1840s brought them west across the Mississippi River to St. Louis for economic reasons. In Ireland, they had experienced crop failures, land shortages, and poor wages. The British, who ruled Ireland, sent over 100,000 Irish peasants to North America in 1847. They came to the United States looking for a fresh start, and they hoped to make enough money to send some home to enable their family members to emigrate and join them in their new country. Thus, after getting to the new world, they worked in factories in cities; some sought land to farm; others worked on the railroads as the transportation industry moved westward into new territory.

According to Dan Sullivan, "The Irish represented more than one-third of all the immigrants to the United States between 1820 and 1860. In the 1840s, they represented close to half of all the immigrants . . . ."[1] In Kenrick's ecclesiastical territory, which included the states of Missouri, Arkansas, the west portion of Illinois, Kansas, Nebraska, Oklahoma, and Indian territory westward to the Rocky Mountains, "St. Louis was the largest city with a population in 1841 of around twenty thousand, about half of which was Catholic or French, English, Irish, and German descent."[2] As the United States was approaching the Civil War, William Faherty notes "66 percent of the Irish immigrants settled in St. Louis" and "a heavy percentage of the Irish opposed secession."[3] Those who couldn't find work in St. Louis got work building railroads in the wide open country. Faherty also notes that even though in the mid-1800s St. Louis had second generation Irish Catholics, the Know Nothings—a nativist political party whose members believed that there existed a Romanist conspiracy by Catholics to subvert civil and religious liberty in the U.S.—"gradually began to identify St. Louis Catholicism with the newly immigrating Irish who lived for the most part in St. Patrick Parish,"[4] of which James Fox was the pastor from 1870 to his death in 1873. The word *Irish* became synonymous "with the recent potato famine refugees," according to Faherty.[5] "The newly-arriving Irish, in turn, tended to identify Catholicism with their own outlook and nationality."[6]

Kenrick needed priests for his extensive diocese. Because he had connections in Ireland, many men came to St. Louis to help him minister to the Catholics—both French and Irish—in his territory. Two of those men ultimately met in Old Mines, Missouri. John J. Hogan emigrated from County Limerick, Ireland, to St. Louis in 1848. James Fox emigrated from County Wicklow, Ireland, to St. Louis in 1849. Both were ordained priests by Kenrick for service in his vast Archdiocese of St. Louis, which, after it was created, as already noted, reached from the Mississippi River to

1. Sullivan, "Irish in Missouri," n.p.
2. Miller, "Peter Richard Kenrick," 26.
3. Faherty, *Dream*, 87.
4. Faherty, *Dream*, 82.
5. Faherty, *Dream*, 83.
6. Faherty, *Dream*, 82.

the Rocky Mountains. A few years after ordination, Fox was sent to Old Mines as pastor, and a few years after his ordination, Hogan was sent to Old Mines as the associate pastor. And there their paths crossed that of the Lamarques, especially Marie-Louise, a Frenchwoman from Ste. Genevieve. It is not difficult to imagine two Irish priests, sitting by the fireplace in the rectory in which they lived, expressing to each other their concerns about their fellow Irish immigrants. Thus, three Irishmen—Kenrick, Fox, and Hogan—concerned about their fellow Irish emigrating to Missouri from Ireland, met Lamarque, who assisted monetarily with the establishment of Irish Roman Catholic missions in Missouri. In the name of Kenrick, Hogan and Fox ministered to Irish Catholics on their farms and in the railroad camps in which they lived, while Lamarque contributed financially to their endeavors.

This book narrates the stories of pioneers Lamarque, Kenrick, Fox, and Hogan, as each in her or his own way contributed to the growth of Irish Roman Catholicism in Missouri. No one would ever have predicted that these Irishmen and one Frenchwoman would have ever crossed each other's path in the oldest French village in Missouri, Old Mines, and in so doing supported each other's work and left her or his mark on Missouri Catholicism. Here are their four separated, but interconnected, pioneer stories.

1

Marie-Louise Lamarque

E TIENNE (STEPHEN) LAMARQUE MARRIED Marie-Louise Bolduc on September 28, 1815, in Ste. Genevieve Church, Ste. Genevieve, Missouri.[1] Lamarque, born in 1785 in Ste. Marie D'Oloron in the Pyrenees-Atlantiques department of the region of Nouvelle-Aquitane in southwestern France, was the son of Bernard Lamarque and Josette Mari.[2] Marie-Louise Bolduc, born May 1, 1799, in Ste. Genevieve, Missouri, was the daughter of Louis Bolduc and Marie-Louise Beauvais.[3]

---

1. *Transcribed Record of Marriages Kept in the Church of Ste. Genevieve,* 201.

2. *Transcribed Record of Marriages Kept in the Church of Ste. Genevieve,* 201; *Washington County Deed Record Books: Book A,* 95–8.

3. *Transcript from the Register of Births and Baptisms Kept in the Roman Catholic Church of Ste. Genevieve,* 45.

Prenuptial Agreement

Before the marriage, Lamarque signed the articles of agreement, a prenuptial contract that the couple entered into prior to the civil marriage which states each party's rights regarding the ownership of property and assets in order to predetermine the distribution of assets in the event that the marriage ends. In 1815, only the richer classes signed articles of agreement. Those signed by Lamarque stated that after they were married Lamarque and Bolduc would be in community in all real and personal estate and property. Neither could be answerable for any debts contracted by the other before the marriage. In the case of the death of either of them, the survivor would inherit all real estate and personal property belonging to both of them. Lamarque agreed to pay a dowry of two hundred dollars out of his own estate. Bolduc retained the right to divorce him and repossess all the estate for herself and any children born of the marriage. Any children born of the marriage would inherit all that Lamarque and Bolduc possessed.[4] This prenuptial contact was signed to protect the real estate, personal property, and other wealth of Marie-Louise Bolduc, who was a minor, age seventeen, at the time of the marriage.

Bolduc Wealth

Marie-Louise's father, Louis Bolduc II, died February 4, 1804,[5] and her mother remarried in 1811.[6] Her uncle, (Salvador) Paschal Detchemendy, who had married her mother's sister, Therese, was appointed guardian for her and her brother, Louis III, to be sure each received their share of their father's inheritance.[7] Marie-Louise and Louis III's inheritance was no small sum when the wealth of their father, Louis II, and their Ste. Jeme dit Beauvais and LaCroix ancestors are considered. Indeed, Marie-Louise

4. *Washington County Deed Record Books: Book A*, 95–8.

5. *Ste. Genevieve Church Records: First Book of Burials*, 66.

6. *Ste. Genevieve Church Records: Marriages, Book B*, 162.

7. *Washington County Deed Record Books: Book A*, 95.

Bolduc and Louis Bolduc III represent the heirs of the merger of the wealthiest families in the Louisiana Territory. Etienne Lamarque, newly arrived from France with only a dowry, became rich because of his marriage to Marie-Louise Bolduc and his entrepreneurial skills of lead mining and real estate.

Marie-Louise and Louis III's grandfather, Louis Bolduc I, made his way to Ste. Genevieve, a port of lead shipment located approximately sixty miles south of St. Louis on the Missouri side of the Mississippi River, sometime before 1765. On January 28, 1765, he married Agathe Govereau in Ste. Genevieve.[8] How and why Bolduc came to Ste. Genevieve is a matter only for speculation. He may have been born while his parents were moving from Canada to the Illinois Country and was baptized at Kaskaskia as so many were before migrating across the Mississippi River to Ste. Genevieve. In Ste. Genevieve there exists a tradition that his father came with him to Ste. Genevieve, after his mother's death in Canada on November 7, 1770.[9] According to Earl Collins and Albert Elsea, Peter Bolduc, a merchant and early settler of Ste. Genevieve, built a house on lowland near the Mississippi River about three miles south of where the current town of St. Genevieve is located today. Within a few years, the settlement was forced to move due to the flood waters of the Mississippi River. Peter Bolduc's house, originally built in the old town, was moved to its present location in 1785.[10] Louis Bolduc I was in Ste. Genevieve as early as 1765 and built a house in 1770.[11] He was among those listed as a "resident of the old village of Ste. Genevieve in 1772."[12] Bolduc wasted no time getting involved in commerce in Ste. Genevieve. He was a pioneer, an entrepreneur involved in merchandizing, trading, lead mining, and real estate. Out of his home he operated a business that today would be called a general store, selling such items as groceries, meats, dry goods,

8. *Ste. Genevieve Church Records: Baptisms and Marriages, Book A*, 131.

9. Tanguay, *Dictionnaire*, 342.

10. Collins and Elsea, *Missouri*, 20-22.

11. *Bolduc House.*

12. Houck: *History*: 1:339-40.

hardware, shoes, stationery, glasses, toothbrushes, fiddle strings, etc. Visitors to his general store paid in lead, salt, and pelts.[13] In the initial inventory taken of his personal possessions on August 12, 1773, following the death of his wife, Agathe, the captain of the militia and lieutenant at the port of Ste. Genevieve, Francois Valle, listed 184 separate items including a feather bed, wooden chests, pots, pans, skillets, chairs, breeches, etc.[14] At a second inventory taken on December 6, 1774, before Bolduc's second marriage to Marie Courtois, his personal property was appraised at 17,459 livres,[15] which in contemporary (2022) U.S. dollars would be over $4,500,000. In 1811, Henry Brackenridge, a visitor from the eastern United States who spent three years in and around Ste. Genevieve seeking an education in the ways of the pioneers, estimated the wealth of the small store owners in St. Genevieve. "There are six stores," wrote Brackenridge, "and in the course of the present year, the imports might amount to one hundred and fifty thousand dollars."[16] In 1811, this was no small sum. At the minimum, Bolduc, one of six store owners in Ste. Genevieve, was involved in twenty thousand dollars of trade a year.

According to Brackenridge, lead was "the fountainhead of all Ste. Genevieve commerce."[17] Bolduc was one of the leading figures of the town when it came to lead. He traded merchandise out of his home store for lead, and he shipped it down the Mississippi River to New Orleans, from where it was shipped to France to be used for roofs, pipes, and to make pewter. Bolduc, in partnership with Joseph Langelier, bought a horse-powered flour mill "consisting of a plot of ground on which it was built, the building equipment, mill stores, and hammers" on March 16, 1780.[18] Langelier owned one-fourth of the mill and operated it for his personal profit for three days with his own horses and harnesses after which Bolduc operate it for nine

13. Franzwa, *Story*, 69.
14. "Inventory," August 11, 1773.
15. "Inventory," December 6, 1774.
16. Brackenridge, *Views*, 125.
17. Brackenridge, *Views*, 125.
18. "Bill of Sale," March 16, 1780, n.p.

days. Repair expenses were divided insofar as Bolduc would pay three-fourths of the cost and Langelier one-fourth.[19]

At some time before 1783, Bolduc became the owner of the Saline Salt Works.[20] Saline Creek, located close to the town, provided lots of salt, which was used in trade and usually brought about two dollars for a sixty-pound bushel.[21]

Besides running a general store, Bolduc was also a real estate agent. There are multiple records of the sale of river-front land with a street on it,[22] and of a plot one-acre square next to the cemetery.[23] On February 5, 1801, Bolduc gave some of his real estate to his children. To Louis II, he gave three acres of land; to Etienne Parent, who had married his daughter, Elizabeth, three acres of land; and to his son, Etienne, three acres of land.[24]

After Louis Bolduc's father, Peter, died, and after the Bolduc house was moved to its present location in 1785, Bolduc enlarged the house. The rectangular building consisted of two large rooms, one a kitchen-living room and the other a bedroom, separated by a central hall. In the hall Bolduc conducted his business transactions.

The home was furnished with the best of furniture and accessories of the late eighteenth century. Bolduc owned coin silverware which was made from silver coins melted by the local blacksmith and made into silverware.[25] In the house were two mirrors and four fireplaces; "when anybody had more than one mirror and two fireplaces, they were considered to be very wealthy."[26] Another status sign of wealth was a chest of drawers; Bolduc had one from the reign of Louis XIV along with a French-Canadian cherry sideboard in the style of Louis XIV. While real estate was valuable to sell, it was usually granted by the

---

19. "Bill of Sale," March 16, 1780, n.p.
20. Houck, *History*: 1:346.
21. Franzwa, *Story*, 69.
22. "Bill of Sale," May 6, 1777, n.p.
23. "Bill of Sale," January 31, 1781, n.p.
24. "Bill of Sale," February 5, 1801, n.p.
25. "Tour of the Bolduc House."
26. "Tour of the Bolduc House."

government gratuitously to anyone who applied for it in order to improve or cultivate it. However, "the wealth of the inhabitants was measured by the persona property they possessed."[27] A legend exists about Thomas L. Maddin (1826–1908), an American physician of great wealth, who offered to wager with Bolduc as to which of them had the most wealth. Bolduc silenced Maddin by requesting him to bring a half-bushel basket to measure Bolduc's silver money, which he kept in his cellar.[28]

Being a wealthy man meant that Bolduc was a slave owner; only the wealthy could afford to purchase slaves. Bolduc's slaves labored in the salt works and prepared lead for transport. They were responsible for domestic tasks, preparing meals, gardening, and caring for the grape arbor and orchard. They also helped care for the Bolduc children. Their living quarters were near the back of the Bolduc house. They were given the Bolduc surname.

Bolduc bought "a mulatto . . . named Francis, about nineteen years old" on July 2, 1777.[29] On July 10, 1778, he bought another "mulatto, baptized Rose, age about 27."[30] "A negro named John, about thirty years old" was bought on December 31, 1781.[31] He purchased "Gabriel, about fifteen or sixteen years old" on May 6, 1782.[32] On July 8, 1782, he purchased "a negress, baptismal name Felicity, aged twenty years, and her son about one month old.[33] A negro, baptized Lawrence, age 25, was purchased on September 18, 1784.[34] On March 16, 1786, Bolduc bought "a negro, baptized Raphael, about forty-five years old, and a negress, his wife, named Frances.[35] On March 9, 1789, he purchased another male slave,[36]

27. "Tour of the Bolduc House."

28. "Tour of the Bolduc House."

29. "Bill of Sale," July 2, 1777, n.p.

30. "Bill of Sale," July 10, 1778, n.p.

31. "Bill of Sale," December 31, 1781, n.p.

32. "Bill of Sale," May 6, 1782, n.p.

33. "Bill of Sale," July 8, 1782, n.p.

34. "Bill of Sale," September 18, 1784, n.p.

35. "Bill of Sale," March 16, 1786, n.p.

36. "Bill of Sale," March 9, 1789, n.p.

and on July 2, 1799, he bought a two-year-old negro child.[37] Bolduc paid silver for some of his slaves, while he bartered with roe skins (deer hides) for others.

Bolduc and his two wives were Roman Catholics, as were most of the French who came to Ste. Genevieve. The town had a Catholic priest, who cared for the spiritual needs of the Catholics living in Ste. Genevieve. The parish in the old town that was flooded was named St. Joachim, in honor of the traditional father of the Blessed Virgin Mary. The church built in the new town was named Ste. Genevieve, the patroness of Paris. Like other people did, the Bolducs, who were short and stocky, depicted Jesus on the cross as very short and stocky. King Louis XV in 1724 had decreed that all slaves be instructed in Roman Catholicism and be baptized.[38] When slaves were baptized, they received a Christian name and the surname of Bolduc; they were married in Ste. Genevieve Church and buried in the Church cemetery, often in unmarked graves.

Louis Bolduc I had a son named Louis (II) with his first wife, Agathe Govereau. Louis Bolduc II was born January 30, 1768,[39] in Ste. Genevieve. Louis II followed in his father's footsteps in business, real estate,[40] and slave ownership.[41] Louis Bolduc II married Marie-Louise Ste. Jeme dit Beauvais[42] on August 29, 1797, in Ste. Genevieve.[43] Ste. Jeme was the grand-daughter of the wealthiest man in the Illinois Country, Jean-Baptiste Ste. Jeme dit Beauvais I.

Jean-Baptiste Ste. Jeme married Marie-Louise LaCroix at Fort Chartres in the Illinois Country in 1725, after which he moved to Kaskaskia, across the Mississippi River from Ste.

---

37. "Bill of Sale," July 2, 1799, n.p.

38. "Tour of the Bolduc House."

39. *Transcript from the Register of Births and Baptisms Kept in the Roman Catholic Church of Ste. Genevieve,* 6.

40. "Bill of Sale," March 25, 1786, n.p.

41. "Bill of Sale," July 5, 1789, n.p.; "Bill of Sale," April 4, 1800, n.p.

42. Also Ste. Gem, Ste. Geme, Ste. Gemme, St. James, and dit de Beauvais. Beauvais indicates the place in France from where the family came originally.

43. *Ste. Genevieve Church Records: Marriages, Book B,* 42.

Genevieve. Ste. Jeme had little wealth, but his father-in-law, Francois LaCroix, a voyageur and merchant, was very wealthy.[44] With the help of his father-in-law, Ste. Jeme became involved in the merchant business in Kaskaskia, which had become a center of trade. Ste. Jeme, "who became the richest man in the Illinois Country, was able to pay [a considerable sum] for a negro family of four."[45] LaCroix lived with his daughter, Marie-Louise, and her husband, Ste. Jeme, until he died. However, before he died, on May 7, 1755, he willed everything he owned to his son-in-law and daughter: "Francois LaCroix: Heretofore resident of Saint Phillipe of the Big Lake, living at the present at Kaskaskia, a donation to Jean-Baptiste Sainte Jeme, called Beauvais, son-in-law, and Louise LaCroix, his daughter: In view of his great age, donates all in return for care during life, his slaves (one Indian man, two Indian women, and a seven-year-old Indian girl) and his branded horned animals at large in the woods at St. Phillipe, also three horses."[46] When LaCroix's will was registered at New Chartres in the Illinois Country on August 22, 1758, there was added the clause that he "wishes to prevent his other children from sharing in his estate, and inventories his property, including three Indian slaves, animals, Cooper's tools, etc. Property not listed in the inventory is set aside for alms and for prayers for himself and his two deceased wives."[47] To add to his real estate holdings, Ste. Jeme purchased property confiscated from the Jesuits in 1765 "being reported the wealthiest man in the western country."[48]

While Ste. Jeme and his wife continued to live in Kaskaskia, he got involved in the commerce and trade of Ste. Genevieve across the Mississippi River. As early as 1754, he had purchased property in Ste. Genevieve.[49] At the time of his death before May 6, 1773, he owned real estate, six lead-smelting furnaces, a water

44. Belting, *Kaskaskia*, 108.

45. Belting, *Kaskaskia*, 60.

46. *Registres de Insinuations*, 83.

47. *Registres de Insinuations*, 112.

48. Alvard, *Kaskaskia*, 414.

49. Houck, *History*, 1:339.

mill and the property upon which it was built in Ste. Genevieve. He also owned real estate with a house, stables, orchard, two wells, salt works, and barns[50]

After Ste. Jeme's death, his sons—Jean-Baptiste (born around 1740), Raphael (born around 1732), Charles (born around 1734), Antoine (born around 1736), and Vital (born around 1738)— moved to Ste. Genevieve, where they owned real estate, cultivated land with their slaves, and engaged in mining,[51] even though they did not live there permanently.

Jean-Baptiste Ste. Jeme dit Beauvais had a wealthy home in Ste. Genevieve. Henry Brackenridge lived with him for a while after 1790 and wrote a description of his house. It was "a long, low building, with a porch or shed in front, and another in the rear; the chimney occupied the center, dividing the house into two parts, . . . each [with] a fireplace. One of these served for a dining room, parlor, and principal bedroom; the other was the kitchen, and each had a small room taken off at the end for private chambers or cabinets. There was no loft . . . , a pair of stairs being a rare thing in the village. The furniture, excepting the beds and the looking-glass, was of the most common kind, consisting of an armoire, a rough table or two, and some coarse chairs. The yard was enclosed with cedar pickets, eight or ten inches in diameter, and seven feet high, placed upright, sharpened at the top in the manner of a stockade fort. In front, the yard was narrow, but in the rear quite spacious, and containing the barn and stables, the negro quarters, and all the necessary offices of a farmyard. Beyond this there was a spacious garden, enclosed with pickets in the same manner with the yard. It was indeed a garden, in which the greatest variety and the finest vegetables were cultivated, intermixed with flowers and shrubs; on one side of it there was a small orchard containing a variety of the choicest fruits. The house was a ponderous wooden frame, which, instead of being weather-boarded, was filled with clay, and then white-washed."[52]

50. "Division of the Beauvais Estate," n.p.; "Sale of Beauvais Estate," n.p.
51. Houck, *History,* 1:353.
52. Scharf, *History*, 1:280.

In Ste. Jeme's home could be found articles produced by the settlers and more expensive furnishings from New Orleans, France, and Spain.[53] It is important to keep in mind that wealth was measured in personal property.[54] Thus, on May 4, 1790, in an inventory of the belongings of Ste. Jeme's wife, Marie-Louise (LaCroix), who died the day before, such items as slaves, feather beds, quilts, pots, pans, candle molds, plates, a China closet with dishes, bowls, and titles to land in Ste. Genevieve and in Kaskaskia are listed and valued at over $800,000 today.[55]

Jean-Baptiste Ste. Jeme dit Beauvais II, son of Jean-Baptiste Ste. Jeme dit Beauvais I followed in the footsteps of his father, who had been considered part of the gentry or upper class in the Illinois Country.[56] Ste Jeme II's wealth is demonstrated by the number of slaves he owned and sold. For example, on August 6, 1788, he purchased a negress named Catiche, age 23, and her fifteen-day old son; a negress named Theresa, age 18, and her six-month-old daughter; a two and one-half-year-old girl; a nine-year-old negress named Genevieve; and a negress named Angelique, age 25, and her twelve-year-old son, Baptiste.[57] Ste. Genevieve Church records indicate the baptism of four slaves in 1761 and 1765.[58] While the slave trade in Missouri is long past, it was a vital part of the economy in the late 1700s and early 1800s. Slaves worked in the gardens, orchards, fields, mines, house, and kept St. Jeme II comfortable.

Brackenridge wrote that he "was dressed in the costume of the place, that is, with a blue handkerchief on his head, one corner thereof descending behind and partly covering the eel skin which bound his hair and a check[erd] shirt, coarse linen pantaloons on his hips, and the Indian sandals or moccasin, the only covering to the feet worn by both sexes, and Monsieur [Ste.

---

53. March, *History*, 1:112.

54. Houck, *History*, 2:269.

55. "Inventory of Beauvais Estate," May 4, 1790.

56. Alvard, *Kaskaskia*, 19.

57. "Bill of Sale," August 6, 1788.

58. *Transcript from the Register of Births and Baptisms Kept in the Roman Catholic Church of Ste. Genevieve*, 1.

Jeme dit] Beauvais was then the wealthiest man, not only in Ste. Genevieve, but in Upper Louisiana.[59]

On January 29, 1770, in Kaskaskia, Jean-Baptiste Ste. Jeme dit Beauvais II, son of Jean-Baptiste Ste. Jeme dit Beauvais I and Marie-Louise LaCroix, married Therese Boucher de Montbrun Sieur de la Seaudrais, the granddaughter of Governor Pierre Boucher, former Governor of Three Rivers, Canada. To this union six children were born. Two of those children are of interest here. First, Marie-Louise Ste. Jeme dit Beauvais, who married Louis Bolduc II, August 29, 1797, and after Bolduc's death married Jean A. Fouquier on April 6, 1811. Second, Marie-Louise's sister, Therese, who married (Salvador) Paschal Detchemendy, February 13, 1798.

Move to Old Mines

Louis Bolduc II and Marie-Louise Ste. Jeme dit Beauvais had three children. Marie-Louise Bolduc married Etienne Lamarque on September 28, 1815, in Ste. Genevieve and moved to Old Mines permanently, although these pioneers were already living there from time to time. Louis Bolduc II and Marie-Louise Ste. Jeme dit Beauvais had a son, Louis III, who married Susan Wilkinson Martin around 1827 and moved to Old Mines. After her death in 1845, he married Louise Reed (Banchard) in 1855. Louis II and Marie-Louise Bolduc's third child, Therese-Genevieve, born January 2, 1801, died as an infant.

Louis Bolduc II was one of the wealthiest men in Missouri (in the Louisiana Purchase). Marie-Louise Ste. Jeme dit Beauvais was the granddaughter of the wealthiest man in the Illinois Country. The heirs of their wealth were the pioneers Marie-Louis Bolduc and Louis Bolduc III. When Etienne Lamarque married Marie-Louis Bolduc, he joined the merger of some of the wealthiest families in the Louisiana Territory.

With Marie-Louise Lamarque and Louis Bolduc III in Old Mines the wealth of Louisiana had moved off of the Mississippi

59. Houck, *History*, 2:269.

River to about forty miles inland. Both of them were in Old Mines prior to Marie-Louise's marriage to Etienne Lamarque. The "articles of agreement" signed by Lamarque stated that the witnessing and signing of the document took place at the house of Jean Fouquier von Pretre,[60] Marie-Louise's step-father; her mother had married him on April 7, 1811.[61] When the "articles of agreement" were written, witnessed, and signed on September 28, 1815, Marie-Louise Bolduc and her brother Louis Bolduc III, were living with their mother and step-father in Old Mines and had been there since 1811. The ecclesiastical marriage between Lamarque and Bolduc took place on the same day in Ste. Genevieve Church,[62] while the civil or legal marriage did not take place until July 20, 1816, when the articles of agreement were recorded in the Deed Record Book in the Court House of Washington County, Missouri. There was no resident priest at this time (1815–6) in Old Mines, and thus the celebration of any Catholic marriage had to take place in the Catholic Church in Ste. Genevieve. However, the ecclesiastical marriage did not suffice for the legal contract, and so a civil ceremony also had to be held.[63]

Lamarques in Old Mines

After their marriage in September 1815 and before July 1816, Etienne and Marie-Louise Lamarque were living in Old Mines. A lead miner named John Smith T—he added T to his name because he came from Tennessee and needed to distinguish himself from all other John Smiths—came to Old Mines in 1804, engaged in buying real estate—as he had done in Ste. Genevieve in 1805— and established a large lead-mining operation. He built a home south of where the current St. Joachim Church sits and, in 1818

60. *Washington County Deed Record Books: Book A*, 95-8.

61. *Ste. Genevieve Church Records: Marriages, Book B*, 162.

62. *Transcribed Record of Marriages Kept in the Church of Ste. Genevieve*, 201.

63. *Washington County Deed Record Books: Book A*, 95-8; March, *History*, 1:115.

sold it to Etienne and Marie-Louise Lamarque. Marie-Louise was now living near her mother, brother, and step-father. Like her relatives and others who had been to Old Mines before her, she was interested in increasing her wealth by mining lead, buying and selling real estate, loaning money at interest, leasing land, and farming. Indeed, she was a pioneer.

Philippe de La Renaudiere had built a small community of cabins for his miners in Old Mines between 1719 and 1720, but because he had no men who knew how to build a smelting furnace, he quickly abandoned the lead mines. Renaudiere was followed by Philippe Francois Renault, the son of Philippe Renault, a wealthy iron founder at Cousolre, France, and a stockholder in the Company of the West (Royal Company of the Indies). Philippe the younger was a French politician, businessman, explorer, metallurgist, forge-master, and a favorite courtier of King Louis XV of France. He left France in 1718 and arrived in the Illinois Country in 1719. He opened mines, built a small fort with houses, a store, and a church—ultimately all washed away in a Mississippi River flood. Then, he moved across the Mississippi River to mine lead on a large land concession given him by King Louis XV's officials in the Illinois Country on June 14, 1723, in Old Mines. In 1733, he returned to the Illinois Country because he could not withstand the attacks by Native Americans on his mining operations. In 1742, Renault returned to France, but miners remained in Old Mines, and they continued to extract lead from the earth.

Etienne and Marie-Louise Lamarque, and before them some of her relatives, had moved from Ste. Genevieve to the Old Mines to add to their wealth by mining lead. Marie-Louise's grandfather, Jean-Baptiste Ste. Jeme dit Beauvais, received a land grant in Old Mines in 1803.[64] The Bolduc side of Marie-Louise's family had been interested in the lead mines from the time Louis Bolduc I arrived in Ste. Genevieve and traded for and shipped lead down the Mississippi River to New Orleans. From Old Mines the lead was transported through the woods to Ste. Genevieve, where it was put on barges and ships going to New Orleans. From there it was

---

64. *Goodspeed's History*, 465.

shipped to France, where it was pressed into flat sheets and used for roofs, gutters, shot, pewter housewares, pipes, glazes on pottery, in paints, in protective coatings, burial vault liners, glass, and crystal, to name but a few. According to John Miles, Ste. Genevieve grew as a necessary port of shipment for the product of the mines in Washington County in and around Old Mines.[65] By 1818, when the Lamarques bought John Smith T's house, the Old Mines village was growing. Supplies could be purchased in Ste. Genevieve. And people seeking to increase their wealth, like the Lamarques, were mining lead. Pioneers were on the move.

On July 29, 1842, the Lamarques appeared in the Washington County Court to defend their interest in two smelting furnaces which they had erected in partnership with John C. Reed. These "two blast furnaces were erected for smelting lead ore with a mill, the cost of the whole being about four thousand dollars."[66] The Lamarques won the case and the court decreed that all right, title, interest, and claim to the land and the furnaces belonged to them.[67]

The Lamarques often loaned money to others to increase their wealth through the interest they charged on the loans. For example, four thousand dollars was loaned to Charles A. Edmonds, William S. Wilcox, and Abby S. Wilcox at 8 percent interest per year to enable them to purchase three acres of land "upon which is situated a lead smelting furnace together with all the machinery and fixtures belonging to said furnace."[68] There is also record of a loan made to John and Nancy Settle for the purchase of some land.[69] Marie-Louise leased a section of land on August 11, 1860, with a clause that all the right to the land was to be given to Edward Robert. She reserved the right to all minerals mined on the land to herself, and she could have any mining done to any extent she wanted.[70]

65. Miles, "Old Mines," n.p.
66. *Washington County Deed Record Books: Book E*, 316.
67. *Washington County Deed Record Books: Book E*, 316.
68. *Washington County Deed Record Books: Book K*, 94-5.
69. *Washington County Deed Record Books: Book D*, 617-8.
70. *Washington County Deed Record Books: Book L*, 469.

The Lamarques were also invested in real estate. Over the course of forty-five years, the Lamarques purchased a minimum of thirty-three tracts of land in and around Old Mines, paying more than $26,000 and selling land for more than $51,000.[71] This total does not include land they gave to the Bolduc nephews and nieces nor the land they donated to St. Joachim Catholic Church.

Some of the Lamarque real estate was used for farming. In a transaction dated April 17, 1852, Marie-Louise Lamarque kept "a right of way through a tract of land so as to pass and repass at all times to her farm."[72] Similarly, on January 1, 1856, after she had donated a section of property to St. Joachim Catholic Church for a cemetery, a clause in the deed states that the boundary line is "not to interfere with the road open on the south side of Madame Lamarque's Orchards.[73]

In order to further their wealth, the Lamarques used slave labor in the lead mines, on the farm, in the orchard, and for domestic tasks in their home. The Lamarques operated what might best be described as a French plantation. Their slaves provided the necessary labor. Some slaves were brought from Ste. Genevieve to Old Mines with the Lamarques, while others were bought after they got there. St. Joachim Church records in Old Mines attest to their baptisms, marriages, and burials along with their offspring,[74] all

71. *Washington County Deed Record Books: Book A*, 395-7; *Book B*, 62, 86, 250; *Book C*, 203-4, 247-8, 477-8, 482; *Book D*, 112, 113, 114, 150-1, 154-5, 217-8, 219, 234-5, 246-7, 335-648-9, 500-01; *Book E*, 1, 13, 26-8, 75, 395-6, 506-7, 589; *Book F*, 86-7, 451; *Book G*, 115, 141-2, 152-3, 183, 198-9, 290-1, 293-4, 315-6, 334-5, 367, 380, 462-3, 539-40; *Book H*, 134-5, 155-6, 258-9, 410-1; *Book I*, 168-9, 197-8, 434, 538-9; *Book J*, 184, 659; *Book K*, 85; *Book L*, 332, 469; *Book N*, 488-9; *Book O*, 262-3.

72. *Washington County Deed Record Books: Book H*, 156.

73. *Washington County Deed Record Books: Book I*, 434.

74. *Baptismal Records of the Church of St. Joachim, Old Mines: Volume I: June 22, 1851–June 20, 1897*, 2, 3, 5, 8, 10, 15, 20, 22; *Marriage Records of the Church of St. Joachim, Old Mines: Volume I: September 2, 1851–September 7, 1897*, 3, 24, 61, 68, 69, 100; *Interment Records of the Church of St. Joachim, Old Mines: June 19, 1851–December 30, 1969*, 4, 16, 25, 34, 39, 40, 59, 81, 82, 89, 160, 175, 186, 223, 260; *Baptizatorum Registrum II of the Church of St. Joachim, Old Mines, August 20, 1820–April 30, 1851, and June 27, 1897–December 8,*

bearing the last name of Lamarque. The French King Louis XV in 1724 had decreed that all black slaves must be instructed in Roman Catholicism and baptized Catholics. When baptized, they needed a last name; slave owners provided their last names for the slaves. Even though the Louisiana Purchase of 1803 had cancelled the Roman Catholicism requirement, the Lamarques continued the practice. Over ninety slaves are recorded in St. Joachim Church records bearing the last name of Lamarque. Thus, with their lead mining, real estate buying and selling, their farm and orchard operation, and more, the Lamarques enjoyed a French plantation home operated with slave labor; this made them equal to any southern aristocrats in wealth and manner of living.

Catholic Church

The Lamarques were Roman Catholics. Roman Catholicism had been the faith of Marie-Louise Lamarque's ancestors, as it had been for the majority of the French in Ste. Genevieve. Etienne Lamarque, a native of France, professed Catholicism. Indeed, Etienne and Marie-Louise were married in Ste. Genevieve Catholic Church, and they brought their Catholicism with them to Old Mines, where there was no resident priest until 1828. As demonstrated by the Lamarques, the residents of Old Mines had to travel to Ste. Genevieve to receive sacraments. The Jesuit missionary Philibert Francis Watrin (Vattrin) from Kaskaskia, Illinois, had visited Old

---

1907, 444, 464; Registrum Baptismorum of the Church of St. Joachim, Old Mines, January 19, 1908–July 10, 1921, 13, 52; Mortuaires de 1836 a 1851; Liber Defunctorum Parochia S. Joachim Loci Veterium Minarum Inchoatus 16 September 1836, 2, 15; Baptisms 1820–1845, Slaves of the Church of St. Joachim, Old Mines, 1, 4, 5, 8, 10, 13, 17, 21, 24, 25, 26, 27, 28, 30, 33, 35, 36; Registre des Baptismes July 9, 1836–July 7, 1847, 27, 32, 38, 41, 42, 75; Registre des Baptismes et Mariages de la Pariosse St. Joachim, Vieille Mine, September 20, 1827–July 9, 1836, 3, 10, 43, 72, 103, 136; Register of Marriages 1836–1851, 72-3, 74-5; Index of the Records of St. Joachim Church, n.p.; Livre de Dispenses des Marriages 1840, n.p.; Parish Census of 1890, 122; Church Accounts, 1885, 107; Baptismal Register of St. Joachim Church, Old Mines, Missouri, 1820–1827, Archdiocese of St. Louis Archives, 13, 140.

Mines as early as 1734 in order to celebrate some marriages.[75] Once he became pastor of Ste. Genevieve, both he and his successors continued to make trips to Old Mines to supply the spiritual needs of the Catholics living there.[76] Father James Maxwell, pastor of Ste. Genevieve from 1796 until his death in 1814 "had come several times to Old Mines, but it was only when he had been called there to visit a sick person or to celebrate some marriages."[77] The number of Catholic settlers continued to grow in Old Mines. In May 1816, Father Henry Pratte, pastor of Ste. Genevieve Church from 1815 to 1822, came to Old Mines to celebrate the first Mass there.[78] Pratte continued to visit Old Mines "every three months until he built a small chapel there in 1820."[79] After he finished constructing the chapel, which was made from logs and named St. Joachim, Pratte visited Old Mines almost weekly.

The Lamarques knew Pratte from Ste. Genevieve. And because of their social, religious, and monetary influences, they supported the erection of the log church and Pratte's weekly visits from Ste. Genevieve. Pratte, born in Ste. Genevieve on January 19, 1788, was the first native priest of Missouri.[80] He knew the Bolduc and the Ste. Jeme dit Beauvais families in Ste. Genevieve, and he knew about their wealth and prestigious social positions. Those family names were held in high esteem and honor by the residents of Ste. Genevieve then and as they continue to be now. Pratte's name appears in the first entry in the records which he kept for the log chapel on April 20, 1820, when he baptized Edward Robert. Alongside Pratte's name appears the name of Robert's godmother:

75. *Ste. Genevieve Church Records: Register of Marriages*, 19.

76. Houck, *History*, 2:297-9, 304, 312.

77. Letter from John Boullier to Bishop [Joseph] Rosati, January 12, 1831, n.p.

78. Letter from John Boullier to Bishop [Joseph] Rosati, January 12, 1831, n.p.

79. Letter from John Boullier to Bishop [Joseph] Rosati, January 12, 1831, n.p.

80. File on Henry Pratte, "Notes: Reverend Henri Pratte, September 2, 1822."

Marie-Louise Lamarque.[81] One week later, Pratte was back in Old Mines for there is a record of the baptism of Andre Jacques Scott, dated April 27, 1820. Along side Pratte's name appears the name of Scott's godfather: Etienne Lamarque.[82] The Lamarque name appears many times throughout Pratte's register.

On September 1, 1822, Pratte died of a fever in Ste. Genevieve. Father Francois Xavier Dahmer became his successor as pastor of Ste. Genevieve. Dahmer continued to do what Pratte had done, that is, make regular visits to Old Mines until July 25, 1828, when Father John Boullier became the first resident pastor in Old Mines.[83] In a letter from New Orleans, dated March 1, 1828, to Joseph Rosati, Bishop of St. Louis, Boullier wrote: "From now on my battlefield will be the Mines, called this because of the large number of lead mines which are in operation. It is a vast territory whose population grows every day; there has never been a resident priest; these poor people have but occasional missionaries at Easter time. There is only a small church in the main village made up of Frenchmen."[84] By 1825, there were two hundred families living in the Old Mines area.

After arriving in Old Mines, Boullier wrote Joseph Rosati, Bishop of the Diocese of St. Louis, officially establishing St. Joachim Parish. He stated that he had received "the care of the parish of St. Joachim, Old Mines, which up to this time was not served by a permanent pastor; as of the twenty-fifth day of July, 1828.[85] By 1828, the log chapel erected by Pratte was too small for the increasing number of Roman Catholics in Old Mines. Under Boullier's direction and leadership, the people of Old Mines began to build "another church made of brick and bigger and nicer than

81. *Register of St. Joachim Church, Old Mines, Missouri, 1820–1827*, 11.

82. *Register of St. Joachim Church, Old Mines, Missouri, 1820–1827*, 11.

83. Letter from John Boullier to Bishop [Joseph] Rosati, January 12, 1831, n.p.

84. Letter from John Boullier [to Bishop Joseph Rosati], March 1, 1828, n.p.

85. *Registre des Baptemes et Marriages de la Pariose St. Joachim, Vieille Mine: September 20, 1827–July 9, 1836*, 25.

the previous one."[86] Obadiah Ferguson (Freeman)[87], a stone mason and an architect from St. Louis, showed the people how to make the bricks from clay found in the Old Mines area.[88] As bricks were made, the building rose. On November 9, 1829, the cornerstone, placed above the double front doors, was set. On the large block of sandstone is carved: D. O. M. (abbreviation in Latin for *Deo Optimo Maximo*, meaning "to the greatest and best God" or "to God most good, most great"), *In Memoriam Sancti Joachim* (Latin for "in memory of St. Joachim"), *B. V. M. Patris* (abbreviation in Latin for *Beata Virgo Maria*; and *Patris*, meaning "father"; thus identifying St. Joachim as "father of the Blessed Virgin Mary"). Then, there are three biblical verses in English: (1) "This is no other but the house of God" (Genesis 28:17); (2) "My house shall be called the house of prayer" (Isaiah 56:7; Mark 11:17); and (3) "How lovely are thy tabernacles, O Lord of hosts" (Psalm 84:1). On January 12, 1831, Boullier wrote to Rosati and informed him that the church was not yet finished because the men worked slowly.[89] The altar in the new church and the steps were carved by Angelo Oliva, a stone cutter and a lay member of the Congregation of the Missions (Vincentians) living at St. Mary Seminary, Perry County, Missouri.[90] The church was rectangular, thirty feet wide and one hundred ten feet long with Palladian detail. The outer walls were built of hand-made brick, the roof was constructed of wooden shingles, and the steeple rose fifty feet. Inside, the church contained box pews with gates, frescoed walls, a barreled wood ceiling, and Olivia's stone altar.[91] Each pew had a divider down the middle with a door or gate at each end which was locked. A family paid annual pew rent, which was used for the upkeep of the church; depending upon where the pew was located, rent could be a few cents to a few dollars a year.

86. Letter from John Boullier to Bishop [Joseph] Rosati, January 12, 1831.

87. Boyer, *300 Years*, 29.

88. Villmer, *250th Anniversary*, 17.

89. Letter from John Boullier to Bishop [Joseph] Rosati, January 12, 1831, n.p.

90. "Western Catholic," 94.

91. Rothensteiner, *History,* 78; cf. Boyer, *History*, 20.

A five-sided apse on the building's west end formed the sanctuary, marked off from the rest of the church by a wooden communion rail. Behind the apse was a three-sided sacristy displaying a window to the north and a window and door to the south; the sacristy was connected to the apse with a double (French) door. A small chimney emerged through the roof of the sacristy to vent a stove inside. Chimneys on the north side of the church vented the smoke from the two wood stoves that were used to heat the building. Each of the sixteen to seventeen windows consisted of eighteen panes of clear glass of equal size with a cross etched across each pane. It had double doors at the main entrance, facing the east, and maybe a side door facing south.

On October 1, 1831, Rosati left Perryville, Missouri, the site of the Congregation of the Missions headquarters and seminary—of which he was a member—on horseback with Fathers Francis Cellini, Francis Xavier Dahmer, John Odin, Louis Rondot, John Timone, Philip Borgna, Angelo Mascaroni, Regis Loisel, and Benoit Roux—all Vincentian priests—along with seminarians Louis Tucker, Frederick Laucier, Hilary Tucker, George Hamilton, and John Shannon. They rode to Fredericktown, and from there to Old Mines, where on October 9, 1831, they dedicated St. Joachim Church and placed relics of saints and martyrs—Sts. Pius V, Venuste, and Honoree—in the altar before dedicating it. Timon preached a sermon in English, and Rondot preached one in French. A large number of Catholics, including the Lamarques, attended the service.

Soon after the church was dedicated, Boullier set to work building a rectory (parsonage, priest's house) for himself and the pastors who would follow him in which to live. The house was constructed directly south of the church. On December 19, 1833, he wrote to Rosati, informing him that the rectory in Old Mines was finished, and that he had been living in it for about two months.[92] The building was a multi-room wood structure with a pointed tent-like roof made of metal. The steep French hip roof's architectural

92. Letter from John Boullier from Old Mines to Bishop [Joseph] Rosati, December 19, 1833, n.p.

ancestry came from Canada and Louisiana by way of Normandy, France, where it was called a pavilion roof. Before metal, such roofs were made of thatch, then wood shingles. The outside walls were clapboard; before that such walls were daubed with mud and white-washed. Both the front and the back of the house had porches or galleries that stretched the length of the house. Around the house were windows, swinging on hinges, for ventilation, and through the roof rose a large chimney to vent the fireplace inside.

Inside, the front section of the rectory contained two large bedrooms, one on each end with an office in the center. To the back of the office was the dining room, and to the south of it was the kitchen. To the north was a large room for the housekeeper, and further north was the small room for the young, male servant who was responsible for pumping water and filling designated contain-ers for washing, bathing, and cooking. A large tank in the attic also had to be filled; gravity fed it to all the places it was needed. The hot water tank stood next to the wood stove in the kitchen; a pipe from the tank ran through the firebox, then back to the tank. The male servant was also responsible for pumping water for the farm animals. He fed the horses, cows, sheep, hogs, and chickens. The building looked like many of the homes in Ste. Genevieve. Boullier's rectory served as the priest's house for over a hundred years.

Church Property

On March 29, 1830, John Smith T, who had previously sold the Lamarques their home and land, sold—meaning donated because only five cents were paid for it—twenty acres of land to Bishop Joseph Rosati "for the sole use and purpose of erecting a Catholic Church."[93] Interestingly, Boullier had already begun to build the church on the land, which had been donated by John Smith T before 1929, but which had not yet been legally recorded in the Washing-ton County Record Book. On April 4, 1836, almost four years after he had consecrated the church, Rosati sold— meaning donated

---

93. *Washington County Deed Record Books: Book B, 498.*

because only five cents were paid for it[94]—this same land with the church and rectory on it to John Timon and John Boullier, the pastor, to "be used for the Catholic Church and no other."[95] Timon was assisting Boullier in Old Mines, and so they were considered to be joint tenants. This practice of declaring the owner of church property to be the pastor (and/or the associate pastor) was known as Trusteeism.[96] The trustee system gave the trustee(s) legal ownership of the land. So, when Boullier, who did not like living in Old Mines,[97] left there in 1836, he continued legally to own the property with Timon. Thus, when the opportunity presented itself to sell the land with "all rights and titles" in 1849, he sold it to Thomas Burke and John Lynch, Vincentian priests, for five hundred dollars.[98] Thus, as of November 10, 1849, the brick church, the wood rectory, and the land upon which they were built no longer belonged to the pastor of the St. Joachim Parish; it belonged to the Vincentians, whose headquarters were in Perryville, Missouri. Within three years of the sale of the church property, Boullier had left the country and had made his way to Tours, France.[99]

When notice of the sale came to the attention of Peter Richard Kenrick, who had succeeded Rosati as bishop of St. Louis in 1843, he, along with the first diocesan pastor of Old Mines, John Cotter, contacted Burke and Lynch and tried to persuade them to give back the church land. They agreed to sell it to Kenrick for one dollar on May 1, 1850,[100] but Kenrick (or his lawyer) failed to file the legal title to the land in his name. Thus, Burke and Lynch remained the legal owners of the church, rectory, and property in Old Mines.

94. *Washington County Deed Record Books: Book C*, 509.

95. *Washington County Deed Record Books: Book C*, 509.

96. Fanning, "Trustee System."

97. Letter from John Boullier from Old Mines to Bishop [Joseph] Rosati , June 2, 1832, n.p.; cf. Letter from John Boullier from St. Mary Seminary [, Perryville, Missouri,] to Bishop [Joseph] Rosati, March 8, 1833; cf. Letters from John Boullier to Bishop Rosati, August 22, 1832; August 22, 1834; August 5, 1835, and January 17, 1837, n.p.

98. *Washington County Deed Record Books: Book G*, 380.

99. *Washington County Deed Record Books: Book C*, 512.

100. *Washington County Deed Record Books: Book M*, 63.

From 1850 Burke and Lynch believed that they had sold the land to Kenrick, who believed that he had bought the land. However, legally it was still owned by Burke and Lynch.

This legal loophole was discovered by Burke and Lynch in 1854. They notified Kenrick that, since they were the legal owners, they had decided to sell the land and file the legal record of the sale. Kenrick immediately purchased the land from Burke and Lynch for four hundred dollars on October 18, 1854.[101] By special agreement the money for the land was given to Kenrick by Marie-Louise Lamarque "for the use and benefit of the Roman Catholic congregation of the Church of St. Joachim in Old Mines."[102] After being passed around for eighteen years, the church property now belonged to the first archbishop of St. Louis, Peter Richard Kenrick, at the expense of Marie-Louise Lamarque.

Pastor Father John Cotter

On December 2, 1841, Rosati appointed Father John Cotter as the first diocesan pastor of St. Joachim Parish, Old Mines. He continued the ministry that Boullier had begun and others who followed Boullier to Old Mines. Cotter was trained at the Vincentian-run seminary in Perryville. While a student there, he worked in the infirmary, where he acquired some knowledge of medicine. He was known in Old Mines for traveling the roads and byways and bringing corporal along with spiritual assistance to his flock. From 1842 to 1845, he was assisted by Father Joseph V. Wiseman, and in 1844 by Father Louis Tucker. Cotter began a Society of the Scapular in 1842. Joining on August 26, 1842, was Madame Therese Detchemendy, Marie-Louise Lamarque's aunt. Two days later, a woman named Margaret, possibly a slave of Lamarque, joined the society.

On June 5, 1851, at 1:45 p.m., while making a trip from Old Mines to Perryville in the company of Vincentian Father Francis

---

101. *Washington County Deed Record Books: Book I*, 179.
102. *Washington County Deed Record Books: Book I*, 181.

Barbier, Cotter was killed when his horse shied and threw him against a tree and then to the ground near Ste. Genevieve.[103] In his obituary, he was described as a devoted priest, whose death disturbed many. He was like a father to his children (parishioners), a sincere and self-sacrificing man admired by Protestants as well as Catholics. John M.J. Saint-Cyr, who was then the pastor of Ste. Genevieve Parish, buried and entombed him in the sanctuary of St. Joachim Church on June 7, 1851. The priests who assisted Saint-Cyr included Fathers Theodore Burke, James Fox, and John Rosi. Later, when Father James Fox finished enlarging the church and slightly raising the height of the sanctuary floor, Cotter's brick and cement tomb became the resting place for a large floor joist! Until 1995, when a bronze plaque was placed on the floor in the sanctuary of St. Joachim Church, no one knew where his tomb was located.

After Cotter's early death, Father John C. Fitnam served as pastor of St. Joachim Church from June 15, 1851 to April 11, 1852. While Fitnam was the pastor, Father Louis Rosi, pastor of St. Stephen Church, Richwoods, had the privilege of burying Etienne Lamarque, who died on November 10, 1851, at the age of sixty-six, after having received the last rites of the Church. Lamarque was buried and entombed in the first St. Joachim Cemetery (Cemetery 1); a grave-sized chiseled marble tomb cover gives his name, identifies him as a native of France, gives the date of his death, and presents his age when he died. In 1852, Father James Fox, who had been pastor of St. James Parish in Potosi, Missouri, was named pastor of St. Joachim Parish by Kenrick.

Before continuing with Fox's story, attention must be brought to the fact that in 1852, Father James Fox, himself a pioneer, was crossing the path of another pioneer, Marie-Louise Lamarque in Old Mines, Missouri, and how within only a few years, they would cross paths with another pioneer named John Hogan. Furthermore, Lamarque, two years later, would cross the path of Peter Richard Kenrick, both Fox's and Hogan's (arch)bishop.

103. *Interment Records of St. Joachim Church*, Old Mines, Missouri: June 19, 1851–December 30, 1969, n.p.

2

Peter Richard Kenrick

Among their list of prominent Irish in St. Louis, Carol Hemmersmeier and Kay Weber list Peter Joseph Kenrick. While they have his name wrong—it is Peter *Richard* Kenrick— they have his credentials correct. He was the first archbishop of St. Louis, he got the diocese out of debt, he built new churches and schools, and he brought new orders of priests and nuns to his diocese.[1] However, as Samuel Miller makes clear in the Preface to his work, "The basic difficulty in writing about Archbishop Peter Richard Kenrick of St. Louis is the absence of source material precisely where one would naturally expect to find it: St. Louis. In the work which follows it may help in understanding it to know that the greater part of Kenrick's correspondence has apparently

---

1. Hemmersmeier and Weber, "Our Missouri Irish Immigrants," n.p.

vanished, not only his own letters but the letters addressed to him as well."[2] However, for our purpose here there is no need to examine extensive correspondence. What we want and need to know about Kenrick can be garnered from other places.

Peter Richard Kenrick was born August 17, 1806, in Dublin, Ireland.,[3] where he grew up. In 1827, he entered the Royal College of St. Patrick at Maynooth Seminary in Ireland[4] to study theology and begin a five-year program of study leading to his ordination as a priest by Archbishop Daniel Murray of Dublin on March 6, 1832 in the Maynooth College Chapel.[5]

In October 1833,[6] he accepted an 1832 invitation from his brother, Francis, who wanted him to come to America. Francis, a priest, had emigrated from Ireland to the United States in 1821 to teach in a seminary. In 1830, he was appointed coadjutor bishop to Henry Conwell, Bishop of Philadelphia. He succeeded Conwell as Bishop of Philadelphia upon Conwell's death in 1842. Francis had sent Peter the money to pay for his voyage from Ireland to the U.S.[7] After his arrival in Philadelphia, Francis appointed Peter "rector of the seminary, vicar-general of the diocese, and editor of the diocesan weekly" newspaper.[8] According to William Faherty: "Peter Richard was a scholarly rather than a pastoral type of man. He leaned, throughout life, towards solitude rather than to the enjoyment of company."[9]

Peter Richard got the attention of Bishop Joseph Rosati of St. Louis; in 1826, St. Louis was separated from New Orleans and became a diocese; its first bishop was Rosati. The pope had a plan to send Rosati on a special mission to Haiti. Rosati suggested that he appoint Peter Richard Kenrick as his coadjutor of St. Louis, and the

2. Miller, "Peter Richard Kenrick," 3.

3. Miller, "Peter Richard Kenrick," 6.

4. Miller, "Peter Richard Kenrick," 7.

5. Miller, "Peter Richard Kenrick," 12.

6. Faherty, *Dream*, 64.

7. Miller, "Peter Richard Kenrick," 13.

8. Faherty, *Dream*, 64.

9. Faherty, *Dream*, 64.

pope agreed. Rosati consecrated Peter Richard in St. Mary Church, Philadelphia, on November 30, 1841,[10] only eight years after his emigration from Ireland to the U.S.! Peter Richard Kenrick entered St. Louis on December 28, 1841.[11] At that time, St. Louis had a population "of around 20,000, about half of which was Catholic of French, English, Irish, and German descent. . . . [H]e found a city still predominantly French in culture, if not in language, with the Irish and Germans making steady inroads."[12] According to Faherty, "He did not share the French background of the largest group of Catholics. Kenrick came as a stranger to an area expansive in attitude . . . ."[13] According to Faherty: "Kenrick lived a monastic routine. At home or away, he rose at four and prayed for an hour before beginning Mass at 5:30. After prayers of thanksgiving, he ate his breakfast. Throughout the rest of the day, he followed an exact schedule of business duties interspersed by prayer. At four every afternoon, regardless of weather, he took a walk."[14] With Rosati's death on September 25, 1843, Kenrick became the bishop of St. Louis, where he showed a great concern for the Irish immigrants, who had left Ireland because of the potato famine and sought work in St. Louis; when work could not be found, the Irish immigrants joined labor camps building railroads. On July 20, 1847, the pope named St. Louis as an ecclesiastical province; it became the Archdiocese of St. Louis, and Peter Richard Kenrick became the first archbishop of St. Louis. Old Mines, Missouri, lies within the archdiocese of St. Louis. Priests appointed pastors of St. Joachim Church, Old Mines, were sent there by Kenrick.

According to Miller, Kenrick's "two greatest needs were money and priests."[15] ". . . [H]e needed more funds for the archdiocese. He had difficulty in supplying his own personal needs. In 1850 he required from each church 1/30 of its gross income for his means,

10. Faherty, *Dream*, 64; Miller, "Peter Richard Kenrick," 25.

11. Faherty, *Dream*, 65.

12. Miller, "Peter Richard Kenrick," 26.

13. Faherty, *Dream*, 65.

14. Faherty, *Dream*, 68.

15. Miller, "Peter Richard Kenrick," 36.

his household expenses, but most churches were exempt from the charge because they were under no obligation to pay the assessment. Only three or four churches gave him anything at all. He revealed . . . that his income for the years 1850–2 was the imposing sum of $451.94."[16] The need for money is met partially by Marie-Louise Lamarque, a resident of Old Mines. In 1845, "[a]t Kenrick's request, John Timon made a trip to Ireland and France in search of priests for Missouri" states Miller.[17] "Kenrick's appointments were heavily weighted on the Irish side. His reliance on Irishmen for bishops and priests was at least in part governed by the necessity of taking whatever candidates were available. . . . Irish clergy emigrated to the United States in large numbers, often with specific training for the missions, particularly the men who came from All Hallows College. The Archbishop of St. Louis was, of course, not the only prelate affected by the shortage of priests."[18] Kenrick's need for priests was met partially by James Fox and John Hogan, both Irish immigrants to St. Louis who were ordained priests by Kenrick. Separate chapters on each man will follow.

On December 2, 1841, Rosati had appointed Father John Cotter as the first diocesan pastor of St. Joachim Church, Old Mines, Missouri. John Rothensteiner states: "For ten years, from 1841, to his tragic death, he was pastor of this ancient church. According to Msgr. William Walsh, 'He was neither a scholar nor a preacher, but he was a most sincere and self-sacrificing man.' Whilst a student at the Barrens [a Vincentian Seminary in Perryville, Missouri], he was infirmarian and thus acquired quite a practical knowledge of medicine. This served him to good use, when he became a priest, and many and many a time by night and by day, did he hasten over the roads of Washington County bringing corporal as well as spiritual health to the poor of his flock. On the [third] of June 1851, whilst accompanying the Rev. Francis Barbier, a French Lazarist [Vincentian], from the Old Mines to the Barrens, the horse on which he rode shied and threw him

16. Miller, "Peter Richard Kenrick," 56.
17. Miller, "Peter Richard Kenrick," 39.
18. Miller, "Peter Richard Kenrick," 61.

violently against a tree. He was mortally injured. He survived, however, for about two days [dying June 5, 1851], and save the words, *Ora pro nobis* [translated: Pray for us], and our Savior's sacred name, which he was heard occasionally to utter, he spoke, as far as we know, not a word. His remains lie buried [on June 7, 1851] beneath the sanctuary of the Old Mines Church. From what you may hear, even to this day from the people of the Old Mines and surrounding country, you would infer that he must have been almost worshiped by Protestants as well as Catholics."[19]

In 1847, during Cotter's pastorship of St. Joachim Church, Kenrick visited Old Mines as part of a tour of his diocese. According to Miller, "At Old Mines, Washington County, where stood one of the oldest French churches in the diocese, the sermon was in English, although Kenrick 'ventured to say a few words in French for the children.'"[20]

After Cotter's death, Kenrick appointed Father John C. Fitnam as an interim pastor of St. Joachim Church, Old Mines, from June 15, 1851 to April 11, 1852. It was during this period that Etienne Lamarque, husband of Marie-Louise Lamarque, died. In 1852, Kenrick appointed Father James Fox, who was the pastor of St. James Church, Potosi, pastor of St. Joachim Church, Old Mines. Fox is the third pioneer to cross the paths of Marie-Louise Lamarque and Peter Richard Kenrick. It is to his story that we now turn.

19. Rothensteiner, *History*, 78–9.
20. Miller, "Peter Richard Kenrick," 44.

3

James Fox

IN HIS 1928 *HISTORY of the Archdiocese of St. Louis*, John Rothensteiner describes Father James Fox as "saintly,"[1] but he doesn't explain what he means. If he intends the description to indicate that Fox was particularly holy in life, his work certainly demonstrates his holiness.

Fox was born in County Wicklow, Ireland, in 1820. He studied for the priesthood at St. Patrick Seminary at Carlow. "He came to St. Louis early in 1849," states Rothensteiner, "and was ordained on June 9 of the same year, by Archbishop Kenrick."[2] He carried with him a letter of recommendation from Francis Haly, the Bishop of Kildare and Leighlin, Ireland, from 1838 to

1. Rothensteiner, *History*, 79.
2. Rothensteiner, *History*, 79.

1855.[3] According to the Lens & Pen Blog, Fox was ordained "on St[s]. Peter and Paul's day—the 29th of June of that year [1849].[4] In the introduction to the Lens & Pen Blog, the authors, Leland and Crystal Payton, write: "Pasted in one of [Bishop John] Hogan's little scrapbooks, in the archives of the Diocese of Kansas City–St. Joseph, a yellowed newspaper clipping has Father Fox's obituary. Unfortunately, Hogan did not note the publication name."[5] However, when compared to other reliable sources, the data contained in the obituary is doubtful (see below). Rothensteiner states: "After doing duty for a while in Carondelet Seminary and at St. John Church, St. Louis, [Fox] was appointed pastor of St. James Church, Potosi."[6] After about six months in St. Louis, in late 1849 or early 1850, Kenrick sent Fox as pastor of St. James Church, Potosi, six miles south of Old Mines. In August 1850, the newly-ordained Fox attended the second synod of the Archdiocese of St. Louis. Rothensteiner lists his name among the priests who were present for the week-long event.[7]

According to the St. James Catholic Church web page, the canonical parish, dedicated to St. James the Greater,[8] was established in 1829; a small brick church was erected in 1831. A rectory was built in 1844.[9] In 1854, Fox purchased land upon which to build the current brick church, a rectory, and a school in Potosi. T.W. Brady was hired to design the church. The cornerstone was placed in 1859, and the building was completed in 1861. According to the St. James Catholic Church web page, the church was consecrated by Archbishop Peter Richard Kenrick[10] in September 1860.[11] Furthermore, "Without a resident pastor at this time," according to

---

3. "James Fox File."

4. "Farewell to Father James Fox, February 14, 1879." n.p.

5. "Farewell to Father James Fox, February 14, 1879." n.p.

6. Rothensteiner, *History*, 79.

7. Rothensteiner, *History*, 180.

8. Rothensteiner, *History*, 731.

9. "St. James Catholic Church."

10. "St. James Catholic Church."

11. Rothensteiner, *History*, 81.

the St. James Catholic Church web page, "the construction of the church went under the supervision of the 'saintly' Father James Fox, pastor of Old Mines . . . ."[12]

After St. Joachim Church's pastor's (John Cotter's) death, caused by a fall off his horse, Kenrick transferred Fox from Potosi to St. Joachim Church, Old Mines, in 1852; he continued to make trips to Potosi to minister to the Catholics there until 1866. He stayed in Old Mines for sixteen years,[13] until 1868, when Kenrick transferred him to Assumption Church, St. Louis. A year later, 1869, Kenrick named him pastor of St. Patrick Church, St. Louis; St. Patrick Church, as described by Rothensteiner, was "the Irish mother church of the city."[14] It was there that Fox died on February 14, 1873, according to a note in Fox's file in the Archdiocese of St. Louis Archives: "Mr. Patrick Fox states that Rev. James Fox died on February 14, 1873, aged 53 years."[15] This coheres with the burial of a James Fox in Calvary Cemetery, St. Louis, on February 17, 1873, at the age of 53.[16] However, according to the obituary in the Lens & Pen Blog, Fox died in 1879[17] Again, the introduction to the blog states: "Pasted in one of [Bishop John] Hogan's little scrapbooks, in the archives of the Diocese of Kansas City–St. Joseph, a yellowed newspaper clipping has Father Fox's obituary. He died February 14, 1879. Unfortunately, Hogan did not note the publication name."[18] Without the source for the obituary, there is no way to check its accuracy.

With his transfer from Potosi to Old Mines, Fox, the Irish immigrant and pioneer, became the pastor of the oldest French village in Missouri and in the Archdiocese of St. Louis. St. Joachim Parish was the church of Marie-Louise Lamarque,

12. "St. James Catholic Church."

13. On page 79 of *History*, Rothensteiner states that he was there for eighteen years, but that is not accurate.

14. Rothensteiner, *History*, 209; Payton and Payton, *Mystery*, 81.

15. "James Fox File."

16. "Catholic Cemeteries."

17. "Farewell to Father James Fox, February 14, 1879," n.p.

18. "Farewell to Father James Fox, February 14, 1879," n.p.

and Fox wasted little time establishing a liaison with her, since she lived in the house which she and her husband, Etienne, had bought from John Smith T located across the road from the parish rectory, where Fox lived!

As already noted above, the Irish Fox began his ministry among the French in Potosi. "Major lead deposits . . . were discovered at Mine a Breton (Potosi) . . . , with a resulting increase in French population," states Russel Gerlach.[19] However, before the canonical founding of St. James Parish in Potosi in 1829, St. Joachim Parish in Old Mines had been founded in 1828. "The early records of St. Joachim Catholic Church in Old Mines indicate that the majority of that settlement's population came to Missouri from France during the period of Spanish control," 1762–1803.[20] "The French at Old Mines, who came early, have managed, more through neglect than by choice, to retain certain aspects of their French culture," states Gerlach in his 1976 *Immigrants in the Ozarks: A Study in Ethnic Geography*.[21] He adds, ". . . [T]he French at Old Mines represent the retardation of the processes of assimilation through both isolation and poverty."[22] He continues: "The story of the French in the Ozarks, from a cultural point of view, has been a sad one. . . . The French proved [to be] inferior to the Americans, including agriculture, mining techniques, standard of living, individual initiative, and enterprise. . . ."[23] Quoting from Carl O. Sauer's *The Geography of the Ozark Highland of Missouri*, Gerlack writes, '[F]or the most part, the French have retrograded with time.'"[24] Again, Gerlack writes: "The only sizeable French stronghold was the Old Mines barite district in Washington County. . . . [T]he Old Mines area is the only remaining French stronghold in the Ozarks, and it is fast fading into oblivion. The French occupy almost solidly an area of fifty square miles, which is centered on the village of

19. Gerlach, *Immigrants*, 11.

20. Gerlach, *Immigrants*, 13.

21. Gerlach, Immigrants, 132.

22. Gerlach, *Immigrants*, 136.

23. Gerlach, *Immigrants*, 148.

24. Gerlach, *Immigrants*, 148; cf. Sauer, *Geography*, 93–5.

Old Mines, north of Potosi. . . . Originally, the French were drawn to the area by the lead deposits. . . . After the lead was exhausted, many French miners turned to farming; some continued to work the surface lead deposits that the [lead] companies had considered too meager for their needs; and few left the area. . . . When the lead mines were almost forgotten, it was discovered that the heavy multicolored spar that had been a nuisance to the lead miners was valuable. This material was barite, or tiff, as it is called locally. It is used in paint, oil-well drilling, and as a source of barium. The mining of tiff became the new industry in northern Washington County, and virtually the entire population became involved in its production and processing."[25]

In 1976, when Gerlach was presenting his ethnic analysis, most of what he was analyzing then was applicable during Fox's pastorship. Gerlach notes: "The French community at Old Mines totals approximately 1,400 people, or 400 families. All of the French at Old Mines are Roman Catholics. Their church in which they take great pride was founded in 1828 and is one of the oldest Catholic churches west of the Mississippi River and east of the Rocky Mountains. There are a few non-French residents in the area . . . However, 95 percent of the population in the Old Mines parish is French. . . . [W]ith the exception of the few outsiders now living in the area, everyone at Old Mines is related . . . . The isolation of the Old Mines settlement has contributed to the preservation of old ways in much the same way isolation has contributed to the general backwardness of other isolated areas in the Ozarks. . . . Old Mines has been effectively isolated from the outside world in two ways. First, until 1949, when the road to St. Louis was paved, it was difficult to get to and from the area. Second, few people from outside have had reason to go to Old Mines; it is a bleak and poverty-stricken area offering little to either the person seeking a new home or the person out to 'see the sights.'" . . . [T]he poverty of the Old Mines area is perhaps the most noticeable characteristic of the settlement. . . . The French in this locale have apparently always been poor; however, they have been poorer at some times

25. Gerlach, *Immigrants*, 148–9.

than others. . . . The high rate of welfare or assistance programs in the Old Mines area is associated with a low educational level among the adult population. . . . [T]he French possess a strong sense of family. . . . This sense of family is a factor that distinguishes the French from their neighbors. . . . [T]he hollows have become settlements, or compounds. . . . [T]he French in the Old Mines area have preserved a French dialect . . . . They are devout Catholics. . . . These characteristics may well be French, but they may also well be the characteristics of a very conservative, traditional, and isolated people.[26] Later, Gerlach summarizes his findings, writing: ". . . [T]he French at Old Mines are atypical of the majority. . . . The French at Old Mines are perhaps the most distinctive of all of the non-German European settlements, both in the details of their landscape and through their sense of ethnic identity. It is somewhat ironic that the distinctive character of the French at Old Mines is more a result of isolation and poverty than a conscious effort to retain a traditional way of life."[27] Later, he adds, "The landscape in Old Mines is distinctive, but, with the possible exception of the family compounds tucked back in the hollows, it is not truly French.[28] And, "The French at Old Mines . . . represent the few non-German European settlements where ethnic identity has been retained to any significant degree."[29]

Fox and Lamarque

With funds supplied by Marie-Louise Lamarque, herself a pioneer immigrant and now a childless widow, Fox began work on enlarging and renovating the brick church that Boullier had built in 1831. Peter Richard Kenrick sent Irishman Father John Hogan, another immigrant and pioneer, whom he ordained April 19, 1852, in St. Louis to Old Mines, to assist Fox; the next year,

26. Gerlach, *Immigrants*, 152–5.
27. Gerlach, *Immigrants*, 156.
28. Gerlach, *Immigrants*, 172.
29. Gerlach, *Immigrants*, 177.

1853, Hogan was named pastor of St. James Parish, Potosi. Thus, were brought together Lamarque, Fox, and Hogan—and the latter two by Peter Richard Kenrick—in Old Mines. Hogan's story is narrated in the next chapter.

To the rectangular church building, Fox added wings (arms) measuring eleven and one-half feet so that the building became cruciform in shape. He used large steel pipes as pillars (two on each side) to support the walls he removed in order to add access to the wings, thus creating three Roman arches on either side. The four original windows, two on each side, displaced by the wings were moved to the ends—the ends of the arms. He replaced the wood shingles on the roof. Inside, the frescoed ceiling of the sanctuary was painted. The simple stone altar was enlarged when the stone was covered in wood, which was stained to look like marble. Three French oil paintings—one above the altar and one on each side of the church—were added. Fox states that Lamarque paid for the paintings, which may have been a part of a collection sent at one time by a French king for churches in the Louisiana Territory or from a group purchased by John Mullanphy when he acquired the crucifixion scene which hangs in the Old Cathedral, St. Louis. Whatever the case, they hung in St. Joachim Church until the 1920s, when they were removed during more renovation.

When Fox was finished, the enlarged and renovated church measured one hundred twenty-four feet long and thirty-six feet wide with eleven and one-half feet wings or arms. On November 12, 1854, the enlarged and renovated church was blessed and placed under the invocation of the Blessed Virgin Mary and her father, St. Joachim, by Father A.S. Paris, pastor of the (now Old) Cathedral of the Archdiocese of St. Louis. Paris was assisted by Fathers J. Caffrey and S. Grugan with many people of Old Mines attending the ceremony. In a parish register, Fox records that the enlargement of the church, its renovation, and the paintings were paid for by Lamarque.

Fox may have also installed a large wood-burning stove in the north arm of the church. At one time, there was also a chimney in the sacristy, where most likely there was a wood-burning stove to provide heat for the priest and altar servers as they were preparing for Mass during the winter months.

It was in the oldest section of Cemetery 1 that Father John James Caffrey was buried by Fox, assisted by S.A. Grugan, pastor of St. James Parish, Potosi, on February 17, 1856. Caffrey was pastor of St. Stephen Parish, Richwoods, Missouri, about twelve to fifteen miles from St. Joachim Church. Like Cotter before him, his horse shied and plunged him into the Meramec (Mineral Fork) River in which he drowned near the Virginia Mines while going to anoint someone near death and to say Mass at a place near there. After his body was found, Fox and Grugan conducted his funeral Mass and buried him along an east-west axis instead of the north-south axis of all other graves in Cemetery 1. His tomb stone was erected by the priests of the Archdiocese of St. Louis; it states how and why he died at the age of forty. "The good shepherd lays down his life for the sheep" (John 10:11), appears at the bottom of his grave marker, along with the Latin phrase: *Requiescat in pace* (May he rest in peace).

Fox began the Society of the Scapular of Mount Carmel on July 16, 1856. Early in 1857, Fox opened a school, built with funds from Lamarque. Now known as the Lamarque School, throughout its history, it has also been called Tin Can University and Teen Town. When it was built in 1857, the one-room school was constructed in the Greek Revival style in an attempt to capture in wood what the Greeks had built in stone. The rectangular building, originally located to the north (right) of the front doors of St. Joachim Church, featured three windows on either side, a window at each end, and two doors near the end on one side. It also had a chimney for a wood stove, which heated the one-room school in the winter. Over the course of its history, the Lamarque School was moved two times by St. Joachim Church pastors.

On November 15, 1857, James Duggan, who had been ordained the coadjutor bishop of the Archdiocese of St. Louis by Kenrick on May 1 of that same year, traveled to Old Mines to reconsecrate the enlarged and renovated St. Joachim Church. Duggan had immigrated from Ireland in 1842, studied at St. Vincent Seminary, Cape

Girardeau, Missouri, and ordained a priest in 1847. Ultimately, he became the fourth bishop of Chicago in 1859.

Even after the church was reconsecrated, Fox had more plans to accomplish with the funding provided by Lamarque. After extending the height of the steeple of the church in Greek Revival style (some of the wood shingles of the previous tower remain under the one Fox built), he ordered and installed a bell weighing 960 pounds and costing $351.30. The bell was cast by the J.G. Stuckstede Bell Foundry Company in St. Louis in 1866. On it is embossed in Latin: *Maria Mater Dei Immaculata* (Mary, Immaculate Mother of God). The bell, paid for by Lamarque, was installed by Fox before September 6, 1858, because on that day he blessed it. Before Vatican Council II (1962–1965), a bell was treated like a person; this means that it was baptized and confirmed. Thus, when Fox baptized the bell, he gave it the name Mary; Francis Portais was its godfather, and, of course, Marie-Louise Lamarque was its godmother.[30] On September 22, 1866, when Peter Richard Kenrick was in the village to celebrate Confirmation for ninety-seven parishioners, he confirmed the bell with the name of Mary; the sponsors were Adrian Coleman and Justine Detchemendy, one of Lamarque's relatives.[31]

In November 1866, Fox opened the first lending library in Washington County, Missouri. With money from Lamarque, he purchased 196 books and established rules for the Catholic Lending Library.[32] Books could be checked out and returned on the first Sunday of the month after High Mass. If a book was not returned when it was due, twenty cents was charged to the person who had borrowed it. Lamarque, of course, was one of the first borrowers of books. In December 1866, she borrowed *Traits for Spiritual Reading* by J. Furniss.[33]

30. *Baptismal Records of the Church of St. Joachim Church, Vol. 1, June 22, 1851–June 20, 1897*, 66.

31. *Baptismal Records of the Church of St. Joachim Church, Vol. 1, June 22, 1851–June 20, 1897*, 22.

32. *Interment Records of the Church of St. Joachim Church*, 43.

33. *Notes*, n.p.

Marie-Louise Lamarque died on July 3, 1868, at the age of six-ty-nine. After burying her on July 5 of that year, Fox recorded that her home was the house of the priest, indicating that he spent time there with his benefactor. Fox explains that she used her wealth for the cause of religion in charitable acts too numerous to mention. All Fox writes is that the enlargement of the church was primarily due to her, its paintings were paid for by her, and the school was erected by her.[34] Because she and her husband, Etienne, had no children, this brought the Lamarque era—at least fifty-seven years—to an end. Only one act remained: the probation of her last will and testament; that story is told in the next chapter.

Marie-Louise Lamarque was buried and entombed next to her husband, Etienne, in St. Joachim Cemetery 1. Her grave-sized above-ground box tomb matches that of her husband. Both are made of marble. However, her marble cover stone (lid) is extensively carved. The first two lines in Latin are a quotation from the Book of Wisdom: "The souls of the righteous are in the hand of God, and no torment shall touch them" (Wis 3:1). There follows: "This tomb, erected over the remains of Marie-Louise Madame Lamarque, silently reminds all who visit this sacred spot to pray for the repose of her soul. During life, she was eminently munificent toward the sustaining and propagating of religion and zealous for the instruction and sanctification of souls. The prayers of those, to whom she contributed, edify by her holy life, and assist by her unfeigned charity, are all she asks in death. She died on the third of July 1868 at the age of 69 years, four months, two days. May she rest in peace. Amen."[35]

In the 1930s, the sides of both Lamarque tombs were taken down due to cracks in the marble—and danger of falling over—and placed under the cover stones (lids). Kent Bone restored the box tombs in the 1990s. A few days after he buried Lamarque, Fox was transferred from St. Joachim Parish.

After Lamarque died and Fox left St. Joachim Parish, the buildings and other things on the property were viewed as being

34. *Interment Records of the Church of St. Joachim Church*, 77.

35. Boyer, *History*, 20.

arranged around the church. Behind the church was what used to be called Cemetery 1, which was moved before the convent/ school was built in 1924 to the cemetery donated by Lamarque, now considered to be Cemetery 1. To the right of the front doors of the church was the Lamarque school. To the left of the front doors of the church was the cistern for collecting and storing water, and to the left of the cistern was the wooden rectory built by Boullier. Behind the rectory was a three-part structure housing the wash house (laundry), the tool shed, and a storage shed. Opposite the three-part structure on the right was the grape arbor, out house, and garden. Behind the garden was the sheep lot. To the left of the three-part structure was the garage, and to the left of it was the well house and the hog house, and behind them were the chicken house and barn. Up on the hill to the far left was Cemetery 1. Thus, with Fox's sixteen years of improvements, funded by Lamarque, the church property was left in excellent condition for the next pastor. Three Catholic pioneers—Lamarque and Fox and Hogan—had crossed paths in Old Mines and, working together, had developed the Catholic area.

Irish Fox was not only busy with the French in Old Mines, he was also on mission to the Irish. Rothensteiner mentions that Fox built a church in Irondale.[36] Irondale is located twelve to fifteen miles southeast of Potosi. The town was platted in 1857 by John G. Scott, who built an iron furnace there. Not only was iron smelted, but lead and zinc were, too. When the St. Louis, Iron Mountain, and Southern Railway (later sold to Missouri Pacific and then to Union Pacific) came to the area in the mid-1800s, Catholic Irish immigrants, who built the railroads, came to Irondale. On August 7, 1860, Scott donated three lots in Irondale to Peter Richard Kenrick.[37] Upon those three lots Fox built a wood church dedicated to the Irish St. Columbkille (Columba), born in Donegal, Ireland. According to records kept in the Archives of the Archdiocese of St. Louis, in 1890, there were thirty to fifty

36. Rothensteiner, *History*, 79.
37. *Washington County Record Books: Book L*, 348.

members of the church. It was closed in or soon after 1909, most likely due to the fewer number of attendees.

Irish Fox also built a church in DeSoto,[38] a new town created by "the construction of the St. Louis–Iron Mountain Railroad"[39] as it made its way from St. Louis to southeastern Missouri. According to Rothensteiner, DeSoto was incorporated in 1857, but the population in 1861 was less than two hundred people.[40] Thomas C. Feltcher and Louis J. Rankin gave four lots to Archbishop Peter Richard Kenrick in 1863. Fox was responsible for the building of a wood church in 1864. In the St. Joachim Church archives, he writes that on August 27, 1865, he dedicated the church at DeSoto, Jefferson County, under the invocation of St. Rose of Lima,[41] the first saint of the new world of the Americas. ". . . [W]hen the Railroad Company placed its machine shops in the valley of Joachim Creek [in DeSoto], the town began to prosper . . . ."[42] Rothensteiner notes: "As most of the laborers on the railroad were Irish Catholics, Father James Fox of Old Mines . . . visited their camps to bring them spiritual succor and consolation. . . . In 1870, DeSoto was established as a parish under the patronage of St. Rose of Lima . . . ."[43] In 1885, the current gothic structure was built, and in 1891, the wood church was remodeled into a school, then later it was removed.

While the undocumented obituary for James Fox on the Lens & Pen Blog has several factual errors, it is correct when it describes southeastern Missouri—specifically Washington County—in the early 1850s as being "country [that] was in the condition of all newly opened territory."[44] The obituary is also accurate when it describes Fox as living on horseback, a true pioneer. Whoever wrote the obituary added concluding paragraphs, which presented the

38. Rothensteiner, *History*, 79.
39. Rothensteiner, *History*, 525.
40. Rothensteiner, *History*, 525.
41. Boyer, *History*, 22.
42. Rothensteiner, *History*, 525.
43. Rothensteiner, *History*, 525.
44. "Farewell to Father James Fox," n.p.

characteristics of the deceased Fox, and must have known him to some degree: "Father Fox was not an orator, and in the pulpit he devoted less attention to doctrinal points than to practical every day advice. He was a plain but forcible speaker, and what he said acquired additional force from the zeal with which he was filled and which made itself manifest in all that he did. He was a very earnest worker; years ago he was the embodiment of the pioneer spirit; disregarded fatigue, and bore up under circumstances which would have overwhelmed many strong men. . . . His charities were uncircumscribed. His health had always been frail, and it was kept so by his forgetting himself in his work."[45]

45. "Farewell to Father James Fox," n.p.

4

John Joseph Hogan

IN HIS OWN WORDS, John Joseph Hogan narrates that he was born on May 10, 1829, in Cahirguillamore, County Limerick, Ireland. The son of James Hogan and Ellen Connor, Hogan was born in the year marking "the beginning of the epoch of religious toleration of Catholics in Ireland,"[1] he states in *Fifty Years Ago: A Memoir*, written in 1898, published in 1907, and republished in 2009.[2] After extensive education in Ireland, this pioneer[3] writes: "I had learned from many reliable sources of information that

---

1. Hogan, *Fifty Years Ago*, 157.

2. Crystal Payton, ed. *On the Mission in Missouri & Fifty Years Ago: A Memoir; Two Irish-American Classics by John Joseph Hogan, Pioneer Priest.* Springfield, MO: Lens and Pen Press, 2009.

3. Hogan, *Fifty Years Ago*, 191–6.

in the far-away Western World, on the banks of the Mississippi, a great diocese was growing up that had immense missionary fields, over which the Church was spreading rapidly. . . . Priests were not needed in Ireland . . . ."[4] On October 24, 1848, Hogan left Ireland carrying a general letter of recommendation from Robert Cussen, Dean of Maynooth College, and arrived in St. Louis on December 26, 1848. Hogan presented himself to Peter Richard Kenrick, bishop of St. Louis, near the end of January 1849. Kenrick accepted him as a candidate for priesthood ordination, sent him to the seminary to complete his education, and ordained him on Easter Sunday, April 10, 1852.

Irish Hogan, "a man of studious habits and fine attainments,"[5] states John Rothensteiner, was sent to St. Joachim Parish, Old Mines, to assist Father James Fox, a fellow Irish priest, who was ministering to the French and getting ready to minister to the Irish, who were building railroads. Thus, through Kenrick, Hogan and Fox were both in Marie-Louise Lamarque's parish together.

After spending 1852 to 1853 with Fox in Old Mines,[6] Hogan was sent to Potosi in 1853 to serve as pastor of St. James Church, of which Fox had been pastor before coming to Old Mines. In 1854, Kenrick sent Hogan to St. John Parish in St. Louis for a year, then named him pastor of St. Michael Parish, St. Louis, in 1855. The "immense missionary fields"[7] began to beckon him during his two years as pastor of St. Michael Parish. According to Rothensteiner: "The Catholic young Irishmen, not finding ready employment in the city, were obliged to seek employment on the railroads, then under construction, and to live in camps, and to move from place to place as the work progressed. This seemed to [Hogan] an anomalous condition, a kind of servitude, from which the ownership or cultivation of land alone could save them."[8] While he was pastor of St. Michael Parish, Hogan com-

4. Hogan, *Fifty Years Ago*, 180.

5. Rothensteiner, *History*, 50.

6. Payton and Payton, *Mystery*, 25.

7. Hogan, *Fifty Years Ago*, 180.

8. Rothensteiner, *History*, 51.

municated his concern about the Irish to Kenrick, who, after Hogan's repeated requests, accepted his resignation as pastor of St. Michael Parish in June 1857. Rothensteiner notes, "Father Hogan . . . did not seem destined to the hard rugged life of a missionary."[9] Nevertheless, pioneer Hogan was drawn to the great prairies in the northern part of Missouri. He was drawn there because the Hannibal and St. Joseph Railroad was being built through the prairie by Catholic Irish laborers. Hogan's plan was to form colonies, according to Rothensteiner, "to which he might draw his countrymen, and enable them to attain a higher standard of living, and a better opportunity of leading a life worthy of the principles they had inherited. . . . North Missouri appeared to him as the proper place for such an undertaking. To go on into the wilderness and to seek a place or two where this work could be mostly readily accomplished appeared to him as the particular vocation"[10] of this pioneer. Hogan's first step was a reconnoitering horseback trip through Northern Missouri in July 1857. After riding the North Missouri Railroad to Warrenton, he was loaned a horse for the rest of his reconnaissance trip through the churchless and priestless counties of Northern Missouri. In general, wherever there was railroad work going on, Hogan found some Catholic Irish laborers. There is no reason to narrate here all of Hogan's experiences, as these are narrated by him in *On the Mission in Missouri*. The focus here is on his relationship to Kenrick, Fox, and Lamarque as a fellow pioneer.

Hogan was not the first to plan an Irish colony. In the late 1790s, Father James Maxwell, another Irish priest, pastor of Ste. Genevieve, ". . . planned an Irish colony in the Ozarks about sixty miles southwest of Ste. Genevieve just beyond Tom Sauk Mountain, the highest point in the region. He sought land for his 'Vale of Avoca' in the interior of Missouri."[11] While Maxwell's plan failed, notes Faherty, "it attests [to] the vision of the pioneer missionary."[12]

9. Rothensteiner, *History*, 50.
10. Rothensteiner, *History*, 51.
11. Faherty, *Dream*, 8.
12. Faherty, *Dream*, 8.

After returning from his fact-finding mission, Hogan presented himself to Kenrick to report what he had discovered, namely, that "North Missouri was a beautiful country, but a land unknown to the Church."[13] Hogan narrates: "And that if [Kenrick] would give me his permission and blessing, I would with God's help attempt to make a beginning there that might grow in the course of time. I ventured to tell him [that] a line of missions bordering on each other from St. Louis to Omaha, should not seem difficult to a missionary willing to make the effort."[14] Two days later, "[Kenrick] called on Hogan, at St. Michael's Church, [his] former home, where [he] was staying for the time being. 'I would not think,' [Kenrick] said, 'of sending you out to North Missouri, on that mission. But since you are willing to undertake it, you may do so in God's name. I give you these light missionary vestments, with portable chalice and altar stone. They are from my own private chapel. I hope you will succeed in your undertaking. But if you ever wish to return to the city I will give you your parish back, or one as good in place of it.' Having warmly thanked [Kenrick], [Hogan] reverently knelt to receive his blessing, and immediately withdrew from the audience chamber."[15]

On September 8, 1857, Hogan began his missionary work in North Missouri by renting the one house in the town of Center Point and converting one of its rooms into a chapel to serve a few Irish railroad laborers living in shanties nearby.[16] He moved on to Chillicothe, where there was but one Catholic woman among the one thousand residents. Nevertheless, the first settler in the town donated a lot to him, upon which later he built a church. "There were no Catholics settlers in the vicinity," writes Rothensteiner, "only a few Irish laborers along the railroad."[17] Hogan decided to establish his residence in Chillicothe.

13. Hogan, *Fifty Years Ago*, 43; Rothensteiner, *History*, 52.

14. Hogan, *Fifty Years Ago*, 43; Rothensteiner, *History*, 52.

15. Hogan, *On the Mission*, 43-4; Rothensteiner, *History*, 52.

16. Rothensteiner, *History*, 53.

17. Rothensteiner, *History*, 53.

After this, Hogan travelled to southern Missouri, near the state's border with Arkansas to look for a place to establish an Irish colony of settlers. The government was offering land at very cheap prices, but most of it was either rocky, hilly, or forested. After getting back to Chillicothe, Hogan writes: "I corresponded without delay, with my dear friend and worthy brother priest, Rev. James Fox, rector of St. Joachim's Church, Old Mines, Missouri, who as I well knew, was deeply concerned for the matter of land ownership and occupancy by Catholic emigrants. The incidents of my late journey, which I related to him, so interested him that he requested to be permitted to accompany me on another such journey, if I should have occasion to make one."[18] Rothensteiner states that Fox accompanied Hogan on his first visit to the south of the state, but that is incorrect.[19] Fox joined Hogan "in the latter part of November [1857, when they] set out together on horseback from Old Mines"[20] and explored southeastern Missouri in the hope of finding a place to establish an Irish colony. Hogan made a third trip to the same area from January 7 to March 13, 1858, accompanied by Father William Walsh, pastor in Jefferson City and another Irish immigrant. Hogan calls Walsh "a loving friend of the immigrant."[21] They discovered several areas which would be suitable for an Irish colony settlement. Once again, Rothensteiner is incorrect; he refers to this as Hogan's second trip.[22] Vacant government land was found about twenty miles north of the Missouri border with Arkansas. After this trip, Hogan returned to Chillicothe to build a church there.

Fox, whom Hogan knew "was deeply concerned for the matter of land ownership and occupancy by Catholic [Irish] immigrants,"[23] bought and donated "a wide and fair tract of

18. Hogan, *On the Mission*, 57; Payton and Payton, *Mystery*, 29.
19. Rothensteiner, *History*, 53.
20. Hogan, *On the Mission*, 58.
21. Hogan, *On the Mission*, 61.
22. Rothensteiner, *History*, 54.
23. Hogan, *On the Mission*, 57.

ground"[24]—in the area north of the Missouri-Arkansas border—upon which a one-story log house forty feet square was erected and partitioned into two apartments, one for a chapel and the other for the priest's residence."[25] Hogan spent from November 25, 1858, to October 30, 1859, on his fourth trip to the Irish colony. It grew quickly. He narrates: "Soon improvements went on apace; cutting down trees, splitting rails, burning brushwood, making fences, grubbing roots and stumps, building houses, digging wells, opening roads, breaking and ploughing land, and sowing crops. Already in the spring of 1859, there were about forty families on the newly acquired government lands, or on improved farms purchased, east and west of Current River, in the counties of Ripley and Oregon; and many more were coming, so that the settlement was fairly striding towards final success."[26] In a small notebook carried by Hogan and kept in the Archives of the Archdiocese of St. Louis, Hogan notes that Rev. J. Fox donated seventeen dollars toward the cost of building the Irish Wilderness church. He also notes that Madame [Marie-Louise] Lamarque donated ten dollars to the church, and a certain Detchemendy, one of Lamarque's relatives, donated five dollars to the church.[27]

On November 1, 1859, Hogan returned to Chillicothe after receiving "many letters from those [he] had left behind . . . in northern Missouri."[28] Hogan was back in his Irish colony from November 15 to December 24, his fifth and final trip to southern Missouri. After returning to northern Missouri, in 1860 he further organized his missions, even publishing a Mass schedule and distributing it to those Catholics attending his mission churches.

---

24. Hogan, *On the Mission*, 68; on page 46 of *Mystery of the Irish Wilderness*, Leland and Crystal Payton write, "Father James Fox was issued a land patent on September 1, 1859, for 320 acres in Oregon County. The Irish pastor of Old Mines . . . donated it for the colony's use."

25. Hogan, *On the Mission*, 58.

26. Hogan, *On the Mission*, 58; Rothensteiner, *History*, 55; Gerlach, *Immigrants*, 43.

27. Payton and Payton, *Mystery*, 48.

28. Hogan, *On the Mission*, 73.

According to Rothensteiner, "By 1860 the railroads had opened the country to an ever-growing flood of immigration."[29]

In 1861, the United States Civil War began and lasted until 1865. Because Hogan's Irish colony was so close to the Missouri-Arkansas border, it was frequently raided by Confederate soldiers from Arkansas, and by bushwhackers and Union soldiers in Missouri. Raiders needed food and transportation. As Rothensteiner so aptly states, "Father Hogan's colony was destroyed, the settlers dispersed, the whole country was a howling wilderness once more."[30] Leland and Crystal Payton write: "Frontier conditions persisted for several decades after the Civil War . . . The Irish settlers had vanished (with possibly a few exceptions), but this considerable area was still called the Irish Wilderness."[31] After the settlers disappeared, the land was logged, farmed, and grazed, and, finally, abandoned. The United Stated Department of Agriculture purchased the tax-delinquent land, when it was creating the Mark Twain National Forest, and congress established it as the Irish Wilderness on May 21, 1984. Hogan never returned to southern Missouri.

First Bishop of St. Joseph and Kansas City

Meanwhile, in December 1866, Kenrick visited two of Hogan's missions in northern Missouri, confirming people in Brookfield and Chillicothe. On March 3, 1868, the pope erected the Diocese of St. Joseph, Missouri, and appointed Hogan the first bishop of the new diocese.[32] According to Rothensteiner, "The Diocese of St. Joseph, in the year of its erection, numbered only seven parishes with resident pastors."[33] On September 13, 1868, Hogan was consecrated the first bishop of the Diocese of St. Joseph in St. John Church, St. Louis, by Archbishop Peter Richard Kenrick.

---

29. Rothensteiner, *History*, 57.

30. Rothensteiner, *History*, 58.

31. Payton and Payton, Mystery, 90.

32. Rothensteiner, *History*, 64.

33. Rothensteiner, *History*, 64.

On September 10, 1880, the pope created the Diocese of Kansas City and named Hogan its first bishop. Hogan was to continue as administrator of St. Joseph until 1892. According to William Faherty, "In 1882, Bishop John Hogan of Kansas City [made a trip to Ireland and] visited All Hallow's to recruit seminarians for his newly erected diocese."[34]

One such man "who volunteered"[35] was John Joseph Glennon, according to Rothensteiner, born in the village of Kinnegad, County Westmeath, Ireland.[36] "After completing his primary course of studies at the school of his native village," narrates Rothensteiner, "he was sent to the Diocesan College of St. Finian at Mullingar, and having completed his classical course, entered All Hallow's College, near Dublin. In this missionary seminary, the young theological student was assigned to the Diocese of Kansas City, and being under the canonical age for Holy Orders, continued his studies under Bishop John Hogan. He was ordained by Bishop Hogan . . . on December 20, 1884."[37] On June 9, 1896, he was named coadjutor of Kansas City, and consecrated bishop on June 29, 1896. Glennon served Hogan for seven years. In 1903, Glennon was transferred to St. Louis to be coadjutor to Archbishop John Joseph Kain, who had succeeded Kenrick. When Kain died on October 2, 1903, Glennon succeeded him as Archbishop of St. Louis. Hogan, a true pioneer, died February 21, 1913, and was buried in St. Mary Cemetery, Kansas City, Missouri, February 24, 1913.

34. Faherty, *Dream*, 140.
35. Faherty, *Dream*, 140.
36. Rothensteiner, *History*, 635.
37. Rothensteiner, *History*, 635.

5

Conclusion

THE DEATH OF MARIE-LOUISE Lamarque on July 3, 1868, and the death of James Fox on February 14, 1873, did not bring an end to this pioneer saga. Marie-Louise Lamarque died childless leaving an estate initially determined to be worth $54,000.[1] Rothensteiner writes "that in his many works of zeal and charity Father Fox was greatly assisted by Madame [Marie-Louise] LaMarque, a long-time resident of Old Mines and a most worthy Christian Matron."[2] In a footnote to that reference, he presents two errors. First, he identifies "Mrs. LaMarque of Potosi."[3] Lamarque was a resident of Old Mines; her legal papers were filed in Potosi, because that is where the Washington County Court House was located. Marie-Louise presented her last name as Lamarque, not LaMarque. Second, Rothensteiner indicates that she "made a bequest of $20,000 to Archbishop Kenrick for charitable purposes, which the archbishop forfeited by not taking the so-called Test-Oath."[4] That, too, is incorrect. Kenrick forfeited her bequest, which was "the remainder, rest and residue to the estate, real, personal, and mixed"[5] and originally estimated to be $25,000, because the Constitution of the State of Missouri of 1865, commonly known as the Drake Constitution, did not

1. "Recapitulation of the Settlement of the Estate of Marie L. Lamarque by George B. Cole, July 12, 1876," n.p.

2. Rothensteiner, *History*, 79.

3. Rothensteiner, *History*, 79.

4. Rothensteiner, *History*, 79.

5. "Lamarque Will," n.p.

permit it. Article 1, Section 13, stated: ". . . [E]very gift, sole or devise of land to any minister, public teacher, or preacher of the gospel, as such, or to any religious sect, order, or denomination, or to or for the support, use, or benefit of, or in trust for any minister, public teacher, or preacher of the gospel, as such, or any religious sect, order, or denomination . . . shall be void.[6]

Following in Rothensteiner's steps, Samuel Miller writes: "The Drake Constitution and its restrictive provisions affected the Archbishop [Kenrick] in another case. Under the terms of the will of Mary L. Lamarque of Old Mines, Washington Co., Kenrick was to receive $20,000 for the education of priests for the Archdiocese. Some of Mrs. Lamarque's heirs contested the will arguing that non-juring clergy were disqualified from holding or receiving property. The Archbishop would not accept the benefaction unless he did so as Archbishop of St. Louis; consequently, the court declared the legacy void and of no effect."[7] Miller is also in error concerning the Lamarque will.

On August 23, 1865, three years before her death, Lamarque issued her Last Will and Testament. In her will, she states that she desires to be buried from the Roman Catholic Church, interred beside her husband, and have a monument erected over her tomb, like that placed on her husband's tomb. She leaves six thousand dollars to her niece, Mary Bolduc, the daughter of her brother, Louis Bolduc III. To her niece Lucy Bolduc, another of Louis III's children, married to Patrick Fox,[8] she leaves nine thousand dollars. To her niece Susan Bolduc, married to P.S. Langston, she leaves one thousand dollars. Four thousand dollars are left to Justine Detchemendy, Lamarque's cousin. To her niece, Sarah Bolduc, another daughter of Louis III, married to Robert Johnson, she leaves three thousand dollars. To each of her nephews—Stephen and Willis Bolduc, sons of Louis III—she leaves $1500. To her "beloved brother, Louis Bolduc III, she leaves one thousand dollars. Lamarque also has a half-sister and two half-brothers from

6. "Constitution of the State of Missouri 1865," 1:150.

7. Miller, *Peter Richard Kenrick*, 70.

8. It is not known if Patrick Fox is a relative of James Fox.

her mother's second marriage; thus, to Josephine, Napolean, and Felix Fouquier Von Pretre she leaves five hundred dollars each.[9] The tenth clause of her will states: "All of the remainder, rest, and residue of the estate, real, personal, and mixed, where of I shall die seized, entitled, or possessed, including herein also everything which though herein disposed of, may be lapse, or other failure in intentment of law be regarded as undisposed of, I give, bequeath, and devise to Peter Richard Kenrick of the City and County of St. Louis, Missouri, constituting him my residuary legatee."[10] In the twelfth clause she names and appoints "Peter Richard Kenrick and [her] esteemed friend, George B. Cole, to be the executors of [her] last will and testament."[11] The will is signed by Marie-Louise Lamarque and witnessed by James Fox and Adrian Coleman.

As already noted above, Lamarque died on July 3, 1868. On July 10, 1868, in vacation of the Washington County Court, Father James Fox and Adrian Coleman, the witnesses to the signing of Lamarque's will, brought Lamarque's will to the County Court to be probated. Erastus B. Smith, Clerk of the County Court, admitted the whole of the will to probate. Kenrick declined to qualify as the executor of the will, because he was living in St. Louis, sixty miles north of Old Mines, and not able to fulfill his obligation as an executor. So, Smith appointed Cole as sole executor of the Lamarque will. On August 5, 1868, during the Fall Term of the County Court, Louis Bolduc III, Marie-Louise Lamarque's brother, along with all those named in her will—Mary Bolduc, Lucy (Bolduc) Fox, Susan (Bolduc) Langston, Justine Detchemendy, Sarah (Bolduc) Johnson, Stephen Bolduc, Willis Bolduc, Josephine, Napolean, and Felix Fouquier Von Pretre—contested the will and objected to it being admitted to probate on the grounds that the legacy left to Kenrick violated the Constitution of the State of Missouri, because he was the Archbishop of the Roman Catholic Church.[12]

---

9. "Lamarque Will," n.p.

10. "Lamarque Will," n.p.

11. "Lamarque Will," n.p.

12. "Transcript: Kenrick vs. Cole," 3.

Lamarque had bequeathed the remainder of her estate to Peter Richard Kenrick without naming him Archbishop of St. Louis. Louis Bolduc III, her brother, contested the will on the grounds that Kenrick was well known as the Archbishop of St. Louis, and that his sister had made a direct attempt to evade the constitutional prohibition by not naming him as such in her will. Louis Bolduc's lawyer argued that there was a principle in law stating that "what may not be done directly cannot be done indirectly."[13] The County Court (re)admitted Lamarque's will to probate the next day, August 6, 1868, except for the tenth clause on the grounds that the bequest to Kenrick was void because it was in violation of Article 1 of Section 13 of the Constitution of the State of Missouri.[14] The court determined that Marie-Louise Lamarque had died intestate as to all estate and property not specifically mentioned in the first nine clauses of her will. The remainder of her estate was to be distributed by the executor—Cole—to her heirs.[15]

Kenrick's lawyer appealed the County Court decision to the Circuit Court on October 4, 1868, and his case was heard on November 6, 1868. The Circuit Court declared that "the order of the County Court of Washington County [which] admitted to probate the will of Marie-Louise Lamarque be vacated and annulled.[16] In other words, the Circuit Court agreed with Kenrick; all the clauses of Lamarque's will needed to be probated.

The next day, November 7, 1868, Louis Bolduc III's lawyer filed a motion for a new trial on the grounds that the judgment rendered in the Circuit Court was not full and complete. Bolduc's lawyer stated, "[T]here was no witness sworn and no evidence was produced in this court that the paper produced, purporting to be the Last Will and Testament of Marie-Louise Lamarque, was ever executed by her.[17] Louis Bolduc III argued that the Circuit Court had not considered all the next of kin to Marie-Louise

13. "Transcript: Kenrick vs. Cole," 21.
14. "Transcript: Kenrick vs. Cole" 22.
15. "Transcript: Kenrick vs. Cole" 23.
16. "Transcript: Kenrick vs. Cole and Bolduc," 16.
17. "Transcript: Kenrick vs. Cole and Bolduc," 16–17.

Lamarque in the case, that there was no provision for appeal from the County Court to the Circuit Court provided by law, and the Circuit Court had no jurisdiction in this case.[18] Three days later, on November 10, 1868, the Circuit Court overruled and dismissed Louis Bolduc III's motion to set aside the verdict and judgment in favor of a new trial.[19] Four days later on November 14, 1868, Louis Bolduc's lawyer filed an appeal to the Second District Court, and the appeal was granted.[20]

On February 8, 1869, the Second District Court heard Bolduc's appeal. His lawyer stated that the Circuit Court erred in not dismissing the appeal, as the Circuit Court had no jurisdiction in the case, there was no evidence to sustain the verdict, and the judgment and verdict of the Circuit Court was contrary to the law and evidence of the case.[21] Kenrick's lawyer appealed that "the judgment rendered by the Circuit Court of Washington County be affirmed.[22]

The case was heard on February 11, 1869. On February 13, the Second District Court rendered the judgments of the Circuit Court affirmed and declared those judgements to remain in full force and effect.[23] Judge William Carter presented the opinion of the Second District Court, writing that the grounds that the tenth clause of the Lamarque will was unconstitutional "was a little extraordinary and entirely 'ex gratia,' [as] the proof of the will had been taken by the clerk in vacation and a certificate granted."[24]

Louis Bolduc III's lawyer appealed the decision of the Second District Court to the Supreme Court of Missouri at St. Louis. Bolduc's appeal was granted, and the Supreme Court heard the case during the October Term of 1869. Bolduc's appeal was on the same grounds as that used in the appeal to the Second District

18. "Transcript: Kenrick vs. Cole and Bolduc," 18–9.
19. "Transcript: Kenrick vs. Cole and Bolduc," 19.
20. "Transcript: Kenrick vs. Cole and Bolduc," 20–21.
21. "Transcript: Kenrick vs. Cole and Bolduc," 22–3.
22. "Transcript: Kenrick vs. Cole and Bolduc," 23.
23. "Transcript: Kenrick vs. Cole and Bolduc," 25.
24. "Transcript: Kenrick vs. Cole and Bolduc," 27.

Court from the Circuit Court, namely, "that the proceedings of the Circuit Court were illegal, because it had no jurisdiction of appeal from the probate of a will."[25]

The Supreme Court upheld the decision of the Country Court. Judge Bliss, in writing the opinion of the Missouri Supreme Court, to which all the judges concurred, stated that the fact that "County Courts, where there is no Probate Court, have original and exclusive jurisdiction in all cases relative to the probate of last wills and testaments is undisputed. The County Court possessed exclusive jurisdiction upon the subject matter of its order, and from its decision there is no direct appeal. The case comes here by error."[26] Thus, the judgment of the District Court was reversed by the Supreme Court, and the appeal dismissed. In the opinion that Bliss delivered, he also stated: "We are not called upon to express any opinion as to the propriety of the action of the County Court, or to suggest a remedy if the legatee is aggrieved, but he is certainly not without one. We only hold that the case was not brought into the Circuit Court according to law, and in entertaining it that court committed an error.[27]

Thus, the case was returned to the Circuit Court, where Kenrick's appeal was. On April 15, 1871, the Circuit Court notified the defendant, George B. Cole, to file an answer within thirty days to Kenrick's appeal before its next term.[28] Cole filed an answer to Kenrick's appeal on September 8, 1871, in the office of the Clerk of the Circuit Court, in vacation.[29] In his answer to Kenrick, Cole denied that Marie-Louise Lamarque had bequeathed the residue of her estate to Kenrick and that the tenth clause was a part of her will! According to Cole, the tenth clause of her will was not made by her when she was of sound mind. Thus, Cole was asking the court to uphold the decision of the Washington County Court to probate the will excluding the tenth clause. Cole testified that the

---

25. "Supreme Court," n.p.
26. Post, "Peter Richard Kenrick, Defendant," 88-9.
27. Post, "Peter Richard Kenrick, Defendant," 191.
28. "Transcript of Missouri Supreme Court Case: Kenrick Vs. Cole," 26.
29. "Transcript of Missouri Supreme Court Case: Kenrick Vs. Cole," 26.

Lamarque estate was worth $100,000. Furthermore, since Kenrick was not related to her, he should receive nothing of the estimated $25,000 that would be the residue of her estate. Cole stated that Father James Fox, pastor of St. Joachim Church, Old Mines, had been a special advisor to Lamarque and had induced her to add the tenth clause to her will. Cole called this undue influence from Fox which destroyed Lamarque's freedom in writing her will. The final point of Cole's reply to Kenrick's appeal stated that Kenrick could not receive the residue of the Lamarque estate because it was forbidden by the Missouri Constitution.[30]

Kenrick's lawyer filed a motion to strike out part of Cole's answer to Kenrick's appeal on June 3, 1872. He declared that some of the answer contained words and phrases which were irrelevant, superfluous, and redundant. Furthermore, the answer presented immaterial issues, and phrases were inserted for effect and not as evidence, Kenrick argued. The court overruled Kenrick's motion.[31]

Three days later, on June 6, 1872, Kenrick's lawyer filed Kenrick's reply to Cole's answer. Kenrick denied having any knowledge of Cole's estimated $100,000 value placed on Lamarque's estate and any knowledge that what was bequeathed to him would be $25,000. He also stated that the tenth clause in Lamarque's will was not due to Fox's influence nor anyone else's influence who had any connection to Kenrick. According to Kenrick, the tenth clause was the free will and act of Lamarque. Kenrick also denied that Lamarque was not bequeathing anything to him because he was the Archbishop of St. Louis, but the bequest was made to him as a private individual for his personal use and benefit. Therefore, according to Kenrick's lawyers, since Kenrick was named as a private citizen in clause ten, there was no intent to circumvent the Constitution of the State of Missouri.[32]

On June 10, 1872, four days later, Cole filed an amended answer to Kenrick's reply. Besides restating what he had already presented to the court, he added that Lamarque had made previous

30. "Transcript of Missouri Supreme Court Case: Kenrick Vs. Cole," 27–31.

31. "Transcript of Missouri Supreme Court Case: Kenrick Vs. Cole," 42–4.

32. "Transcript of Missouri Supreme Court Case: Kenrick Vs. Cole," 45–9.

wills before the adoption of the then-present Missouri Constitution on July 4, 1865, which named Kenrick as Archbishop of St. Louis as her residuary legatee. He declared that after the adoption of the Missouri Constitution in 1865, Lamarque changed her will in order to avoid Section 13, Article 1, by naming Kenrick without his ecclesiastical title; her intention was the same as in her previous wills,[33] namely, that "Kenrick should take the legacy given by said pretended tenth clause and use it as archbishop for educational purposes and for the repair of the church house of the Roman Catholic Church at Old Mines."[34] On the same day, Kenrick's lawyer filed a motion to have parts of Cole's amended answer struck from the record,[35] but the court made no reply because the parties had filed for a change of venue from the Circuit Court of Washington County to the Circuit Court of St. Louis County, and the change of venue was granted.[36]

The Circuit Court of St. Louis County, Eighth Judicial Circuit, heard the case on June 17, 1873. While Cole had filed another answer to Kenrick's amended reply,[37] he introduced no new evidence into the case. On January 5, 1874, the Circuit Court rendered its decision: "[T]he tenth clause in . . . Marie-Louise Lamarque's last will is not a part of her last will as alleged. Therefore, it is considered by the court that the . . . tenth clause contained in the last will of Marie-Louise Lamarque, deceased, is not a part of the last will and testament of . . . Marie-Louise Lamarque as alleged."[38] This meant that whatever was left of Lamarque's estate would be distributed among the other people named in the other clauses of her will; Kenrick would receive nothing.

Thus, Kenrick's lawyer filed a motion for a new trial on February 13, 1874, and that motion was denied.[39] However, on March

33. "Transcript of Missouri Supreme Court Case: Kenrick Vs. Cole," 49–50.
34. "Transcript of Missouri Supreme Court Case: Kenrick Vs. Cole," 53.
35. "Transcript of Missouri Supreme Court Case: Kenrick Vs. Cole," 54–9.
36. "Transcript of Missouri Supreme Court Case: Kenrick Vs. Cole," 60–61.
37. "Transcript of Missouri Supreme Court Case: Kenrick Vs. Cole," 63–5.
38. "Transcript of Missouri Supreme Court Case: Kenrick Vs. Cole," 66–7.
39. "Transcript of Missouri Supreme Court Case: Kenrick Vs. Cole," 67.

9, 1874, an appeal was granted to him during the General Term of the Circuit Court of St. Louis County. During the appeal, the one-time physician of Lamarque, Doctor William Evans, testified for Cole stating that Lamarque "was a very feeble woman, suffering from rheumatism and perioditus (sic) for years. For the last few years she was unable to leave the house or go to church. The most she could do was to walk to the breakfast table. For years before her death it would not have been prudent for Mrs. Lamarque to have been left alone."[40] Cole testified: "As executor of Mrs. Lamarque, I judge that the value of the estate including everything, real as well as personal property is $50,000 [to] $35,000 in bonds and notes, $12,000 to $15,000 in real estate, and $130 in money—$7,000, part of the above, was in Boatman's Bank. Mrs. Lamarque was a lady of feeble health and it would not have been safe for her to live alone, so that Miss Detchemendy and Miss Bolduc resided with her. Her mind was not impaired, though she was very old. She was no relative of Archbishop Kenrick, either by blood or marriage. I have seen Father Fox at her house."[41]

The defense then read a deposition of Fox which had been made by him on September 29, 1871, in St. Louis two years before he had died. In the deposition, Fox stated that Lamarque left a will and that he was one of the witnesses of it. He noted that Lamarque had made four wills, the last one having been made after the new Constitution of the State of Missouri went into effect. He stated that he remembered that in the tenth clause of her last will, Lamarque had made Kenrick her residuary legatee. He also remembered that for five years or more before her death that Lamarque was in poor health, afflicted with rheumatism, but her mind was sound and clear to the last. Fox testified that he was well acquainted with Lamarque, that he was at her house and in her company frequently—almost every day—during the time he lived in Old Mines.[42] Specifically, Fox stated: "There was a considerable legacy bequeathed to the archbishop for educational purposes, principally for the education

40. "Transcript of Missouri Supreme Court Case: Kenrick Vs. Cole," 68–9.
41. "Transcript of Missouri Supreme Court Case: Kenrick Vs. Cole," 69–70.
42. "Transcript of Missouri Supreme Court Case: Kenrick Vs. Cole," 71–2.

of the children at Old Mines; he had a right by that will to expend a portion of the legacy for the repairs of the church at Old Mines if he thought proper. The object of making a new will, now her last will, was to avoid and preclude the possibility of litigation under the new, the present, Constitution of the State of Missouri. In my presence and in her own room, Mrs. Lamarque requested and Mr. Louis Bolduc [III], her brother, promised her that he would not in any way interfere with her will. She said that her intention in making Peter Richard Kenrick residuary legatee was the same as when she bequeathed him a certain amount in her former will as Archbishop of St. Louis. In her last will she left it to him as a citizen and an individual and left the disposition of it to his own judgment and discretion. However, we all know she would not have made him her residuary legatee had he not been archbishop of St. Louis and a Catholic clergyman."[43]

In his deposition, Fox reported that he had notified Kenrick about the tenth clause in her will after Lamarque's death, and Kenrick had told him that he would defend the tenth clause on the principle that he was made residuary in his capacity as a citizen and a private individual. Fox also reported that Kenrick had said that he would accept the bequest and that he would act according to Lamarque's wishes.[44]

Alex J.P. Garesche, who wrote (prepared) Lamarque's wills, stated that in a former will, Lamarque left Kenrick four thousand dollars for the Catholic Church in Old Mines and that the remainder of her estate was willed to him for charitable and education purposes. Also, there was a small sum left to him personally, said Garesche. After the adoption of the new Constitution for the State of Missouri, satisfied that its clause was aimed especially against the Catholic Church and its ownership of property in the state, Garesche wrote (prepared) Lamarque's will, but he feared that the residuary tenth clause of her will would be annulled by the constitution. So, after notifying her and with her approval, he wrote the last will, excluding every idea of trust and not giving

43. "Transcript of Missouri Supreme Court Case: Kenrick Vs. Cole," 72–3.
44. "Transcript of Missouri Supreme Court Case: Kenrick Vs. Cole," 75.

any title to Kenrick. He explained that his reasoning was that the archbishop could receive the residue individually and personally, but not as archbishop.[45]

Kenrick, testifying on his behalf, stated that he had made no definite promise to Lamarque. However, he remembered three of her intentions in her former wills: (1) Religious services for her after her death, (2) relief of the poor of the church at Old Mines, and (3) for the theological seminary in St. Louis. He thought that six thousand dollars had been left by Lamarque to the seminary for the education of young men for the priesthood and that ten thousand dollars had been left by her for Masses for the repose of her soul to be said in Old Mines. Kenrick closed with a statement in which he reported that he had told Fox that he wanted to be able to accept Lamarque's bequest under the new constitution, and that he would abide by her intentions. He said, "The change of the will was a matter of form to make it in accordance with law."[46]

After all the evidence was presented and everyone had testified, the Circuit Court of St. Louis County ruled that the tenth clause of the Lamarque will could not be probated because Lamarque's intention—being the same as in her previous wills—was contrary to the Missouri Constitution.[47] Kenrick's lawyer made a motion for a new trial, but the motion was denied.[48] Nevertheless, On March 25, 1874, Kenrick's lawyer filed for an appeal, and the court granted him an appeal to the Missouri Supreme Court.[49]

The Missouri Supreme Court heard the case in its January term of 1876. Judge Wagner delivered the opinion of the court, writing, "[T]he court found that the tenth clause was made for an illegal purpose and with the intent to evade the prohibitions of the constitution."[50] He also said that it was an attempt to do indirectly what was directly forbidden. Wagner wrote that Kenrick

45. "Transcript of Missouri Supreme Court Case: Kenrick Vs. Cole," 76–7.
46. "Transcript of Missouri Supreme Court Case: Kenrick Vs. Cole," 78–9.
47. "Transcript of Missouri Supreme Court Case: Kenrick Vs. Cole," 80–83.
48. "Transcript of Missouri Supreme Court Case: Kenrick Vs. Cole," 45–9.
49. "Transcript of Missouri Supreme Court Case: Kenrick Vs. Cole," 85.
50. Post, "Peter Richard Kenrick, Appellant," 576.

could have held the property for his own use, but he had stated that if he obtained it, he would carry out Lamarque's wishes. "If this were allowed, the prohibiting law would be a nullity. It would place the property in possession of the church in defiance of the constitution."[51] Thus, the judgement of the Washington County Court was upheld, and the case was dismissed. The will was to be probated without the tenth clause.

As this case was making its way through the courts, Cole, executor of Lamarque's will, was making settlements. After the $28,500 specifically designated in her will to individuals was distributed, the remainder of her estate amounted to $54,247.24.[52] That remainder was divided by Cole and given to her heirs named in her will.

Before Cole was dismissed as executor on November 17, 1876, he had made seventeen settlements concerning the Lamarque will.[53] The Lamarques, who had been supporters of the Catholic Church for over fifty years and pioneers in southern Missouri, were unable to leave anything to the church because of Section 13, Article 1 of the 1865 Missouri Constitution. Neither Archbishop Peter Richard Kenrick nor St. Joachim Church, Old Mines, received anything of the residue of the state of Marie-Louise Lamarque!

The burial places of Etienne and Marie-Louise Lamarque in Cemetery 1 further confirm their wealth. The burial custom of the wealthy French was burial in the ground with a large vault above ground and a monument-stone on top of the vault. In Ste. Genevieve, the vaults for the Bolduc and Ste. Jeme dit Beauvais families serve as attestation to the families' wealth. In all of Old Mines, there are only four such vaults, one over Etienne Lamarque and one over Marie-Louis Lamarque, his wife. The other two vaults are over Louis Bolduc III, Marie-Louis Lamarque's brother, who contested her will, and over his first wife, Susan Wilkinson Martin.

51. Post, "Peter Richard Kenrick, Appellant," 577.

52. "Recapitulation of the Settlement of the Estate of Marie L. Lamarque by George B. Cole, July 12, 1876," n.p.

53. "Recapitulation of the Settlement of the Estate of Marie L Lamarque," 269, 363, 403.

Conclusion

Considering all of Marie-Louise Lamarque's other monetary donations to St. Joachim Catholic Church, it is not difficult to consider that she may have bought the land known today as the Irish Wilderness, that is, she may have given the money to Fox to pay for the thee-hundred twenty acres in Oregon County. Because her monetary munificence is so well attested, she may have purchased the land through Fox for Hogan's Irish colony.

Kenrick's loss of over $54,000 would have made Lamarque, the financial pioneer she was, roll over in her grave! It is clear from the court records that she intended Kenrick to have the money for purposes she had intended. The Missouri Constitution of 1865 (Drake Constitution) put a stumbling block in her way. Either she or, more likely, her lawyer thought they had devised a way around the prohibition of that constitution by separating Kenrick as a citizen from his ecclesiastical position as archbishop. However, the Missouri Supreme Court recognized that such separation was not possible. Even though the will had been changed to conform to the law, it attempted to do indirectly (bequeath money to a clergyman without naming him as such) what could not be done directly (bequeath money to a clergyman by name).

To have broken his promise not to contest his sister's will leaves a black mark on Louis Bolduc III and all those who joined him in contesting Marie-Louise (Bolduc) Lamarque's will. Louis Bolduc III presents himself as greedy. He was already coheir with his sister to the fortunes of the richest people in the Louisiana Purchase having lived in Ste. Genevieve, Missouri. It is obvious that he did not share his sister's religious values, especially her financial support for Catholic pioneers. Furthermore, it seems obvious that he did not want Kenrick to receive anything that Lamarque bequeathed to him, and he was willing to go all the way to the Missouri Supreme Court two times to be sure that it did not happen. Louis Bolduc III was a permanent resident of Old Mines with none of the pioneer spirit that possessed his sister and

Fox. Lamarque was the financial pioneer behind the ecclesiastical pioneering of Fox and, most likely, Hogan.

Kenrick died on March 4, 1896, twenty years after the legal battle over Lamarque's will. Both Rothensteiner and Faherty in their histories narrate all the pioneering Kenrick did in St. Louis and beyond. After all, it was his desire that his archdiocese be subdivided into smaller dioceses, like that given to John Hogan. It was Kenrick who sent Fox to St. Joachim Church as pastor, and Kenrick who sent Hogan there as Fox's associate. Fox's enlarged church at Lamarque's expense, continues even today to serve the Roman Catholics living in the oldest village in the State of Missouri. Other modern pioneers from various ethnic backgrounds around the world, including the United States, have since moved into the French village area of Old Mines, where there are no more pioneers like the Lamarques, Kenrick, Fox, or Hogan.

After the Civil War ended, Hogan gave up on taming the frontier conditions in southern Missouri with a colony of Irish immigrants. The Irish Wilderness, a part of the Mark Twain National Forest, still contains a few remnants of house foundations, store foundations, a mill wheel, etc. that can be seen by those backpackers exploring the area and that attest to the presence of the Irish colony there for a few years. Hogan focused his attention after the Civil War on northern Missouri, where he followed Irish railroad laborers and established Catholic Churches for them in the towns in which they settled. His appointment as first bishop of the Diocese of St. Joseph in 1869 confirmed his pioneer work, and his appointment as first bishop of the Diocese of Kansas City, Missouri, in 1880 further confirmed it. He continued to build churches and open cathedrals in territory quickly filling with people from many different ethnic backgrounds, including Irish.

In the middle of the nineteenth century, the paths of four people—three Irish and one French—crossed and crisscrossed paths in Old Mines, Missouri, and their Catholic pioneer spirit continues to exist among those who live in the oldest settlement in the State of Missouri.

Bibliography

Alvard, Clarence Walworth. *Kaskaskia Records: 1778–1790*. Virginia Series II. Springfield, IL: Illinois State Historical Library, 1909.

Baptismal Records of the Church of St. Joachim, Old Mines: Volume I: June 22, 1851–June 20, 1897. Old Mines, MO: n.p.

Baptisms 1820–1845, Slaves of the Church of St. Joachim, Old Mines. Old Mines, MO: n.p.

Baptismal Register of St. Joachim Church, Old Mines, Missouri, 1820–1827. St. Louis, MO: Archdiocese of St. Louis Archives, n.p.

Baptizatorum Registrum II of the Church of St. Joachim, Old Mines, August 20, 1820–April 30, 1851, and June 27, 1897–December 8, 1907. Old Mines, MO: n.p.

Belting, Natalia Maree. *Kaskaskia under the French Regime*. 3 vols. Urbana, IL: University of Illinois Press, 1948.

"Bill of Sale." May 6, 1777. Ste. Genevieve, MO: Ste. Genevieve Court House Archives, n.p.

"Bill of Sale." July 2, 1777. Ste. Genevieve, MO: Ste. Genevieve Court House Archives, n.p.

"Bill of Sale." July 10, 1778. Ste. Genevieve, MO: Ste. Genevieve Court House Archives, n.p.

"Bill of Sale." March 16, 1780. Ste. Genevieve, MO: Ste. Genevieve Court House Archives, n.p.

"Bill of Sale." January 31, 1781. Ste. Genevieve, MO: Ste. Genevieve Court House Archives, n.p.

"Bill of Sale." December 31, 1781. Ste. Genevieve, MO: Ste. Genevieve Court House Archives, n.p.

"Bill of Sale." May 6, 1782. Ste. Genevieve, MO: Ste. Genevieve Court House Archives, n.p.

"Bill of Sale." July 8, 1782. Ste. Genevieve, MO: Ste. Genevieve Court House Archives, n.p.

"Bill of Sale." September 18, 1784. Ste. Genevieve, MO: Ste. Genevieve Court House Archives, n.p.

"Bill of Sale." March 16, 1786. Ste. Genevieve, MO: Ste. Genevieve Court House Archives, n.p.

"Bill of Sale." March 25, 1786. Ste. Genevieve, MO: Ste. Genevieve Court House Archives, n.p.

"Bill of Sale." August 6, 1788. Ste. Genevieve, MO: Ste. Genevieve Court House Archives, n.p.

"Bill of Sale." March 9, 1789. Ste. Genevieve, MO: Ste. Genevieve Court House Archives, n.p.

"Bill of Sale." July 5, 1789. Ste. Genevieve, MO: Ste. Genevieve Court House Archives, n.p.

"Bill of Sale." July 2, 1799. Ste. Genevieve, MO: Ste. Genevieve Court House Archives, n.p.

"Bill of Sale." April 4, 1800. Ste. Genevieve, MO: Ste. Genevieve Court House Archives, n.p.

"Bill of Sale." February 5, 1801. Ste. Genevieve, MO: Ste. Genevieve Court House Archives, n.p.

The Bolduc House. Washington, DC: National Society of the Colonial Dames in America, n.p.

Boyer, Mark G. *History of St. Joachim Parish: 1822–1972; 1723–1973.* Kansas City, MO: Yearbook House, 1972.

———. *300 Years of the French in Old Mines: A Narrative History of the Oldest Village in Missouri.* Eugene, OR: Wipf and Stock, 2021.

Brackenridge, Henry M. *Views of Louisiana; Together with a Journal of a Voyage up the Mississippi River, in 1811.* Pittsburgh, PA: Cramer, Spear, and Eichbaum, 1811.

"Catholic Cemeteries," Archdiocese of St. Louis. https://archstl.org/catholic-cemeteries; https://awaittheblessedhope.org/burial-search.

Church Accounts, 1885. St. Joachim Church, Old Mines, MO: n.p.

Collins, Earl A. and Albert F. Elsea. *Missouri: Its People and Its Progress.* St. Louis: Webster, 1940.

"Constitution of the State of Missouri 1865." In *Vernon's Annotated Missouri Statutes.* Volume 1. St. Paul, MN: West Publishing Company, 1970.

"Division of Beauvais Estate." May 6, 1773. Ste. Genevieve, MO: Ste. Genevieve Court House Archives, n.p.

Faherty, William B. *Dream by the River: Two Centuries of Saint Louis Catholicism 1766–1980.* St. Louis: River City, 1981.

Fanning, William H.W. "Trustee System." In *The Catholic Encyclopedia* 25:71-2. New York, NY: Encyclopedia Press, 1913.

"Farewell to Father James Fox, February 14, 1879." Lens & Pen Blog. http://lensandpen.blogspot.com/2015/02/farewell-to-father-james-fox-february.html.

File on Henry Pratte, "Notes: Reverend Henri Pratte, September 2, 1822." St. Louis, MO: Archives of the Archdiocese of St. Louis, n.p.

Franzwa, Gregory M. *The Story of Old Ste. Genevieve.* St. Louis, MO: Patrice, 1967.

Gerlach, Russel. *Immigrants in the Ozarks: A Study in Ethnic Geography.* Columbia, MO: University of Missouri Press, 1976.

Goodspeed's History of Franklin, Jefferson, Washington, Crawford, and Gasconade Counties, Missouri. Cape Girardeau, MO: Ramfre, 1888.

Hemmersmeier, Carol, and Kay Weber. "Our Missouri Irish Immigrants." St. Louis Genealogical Society Family History Conference. May 2, 2021. https://stlgs.org/media/pdf/missouri-irish-immigrants-weber-2021.pdf.

Hogan, John. J. *On the Mission in Missouri 1857–1868.* Springfield, MO: Lens & Penn, 2009

———. *Fifty Years Ago: A Memoir.* Springfield, MO: Lens & Penn, 2009.

Houck, Louis. *A History of Missouri: 3 vols.* Chicago, IL: R.R. Donnelly and Sons, 1908.

Index of the Records of St. Joachim Church. Old Mines, MO: n.p.

Interment Records of the Church of St. Joachim, Old Mines: June 19, 1851– December 30, 1969. Old Mines, MO: n.p.

"Inventory of Beauvais Estate." Ste. Genevieve, MO: St. Genevieve Court House Archives, May 4, 1790.

"Inventory of Bolduc Estate." Ste. Genevieve, MO: Ste. Genevieve Court House Archives, August 11, 1773.

"Inventory of Bolduc Estate." Ste. Genevieve, MO: St. Genevieve Court House Archives, December 6, 1774.

"James Fox File." St. Louis, MO: Archives of the Archdiocese of St. Louis, n.p.

"Lamarque Will." *Washington County Will Record Books: Book C.* Potosi, MO: Washington County Court House, n.p.

"Lens & Pen Blog." http://lensandpen.blogspot.com/2015/02/farwell-to-father-james-fox-february.html.

Letter from John Boullier [from New Orleans, LA, to Bishop Joseph Rosati], March 1, 1828. St. Louis, MO: Archives of the Archdiocese of St. Louis, n.p.

Letter from John Boullier [from Old Mines, Missouri] to Bishop [Joseph] Rosati [in St. Louis, Missouri], January 12, 1831. St. Louis, MO: Archives of the Archdiocese of St. Louis, n.p.

Letter from John Boullier from Old Mines [, Missouri,] to Bishop [Joseph] Rosati [in St. Louis, Missouri], June 12, 1831. St. Louis, MO: Archives of the Archdiocese of St. Louis, n.p.

Letter from John Boullier from Old Mines [, Missouri,] to Bishop [Joseph] Rosati [in St. Louis, Missouri], June 2, 1832. St. Louis, MO: Archives of the Archdiocese of St. Louis, n.p.

Letter from John Boullier to Bishop Rosati, August 22, 1832. St. Louis, MO: Archives of the Archdiocese of St. Louis, n.p.

Letter from John Boullier from St. Mary Seminary [, Perryville, Missouri,] to Bishop [Joseph] Rosati [in St. Louis, Missouri], March 8, 1833.

Letter from John Boullier from Old Mines [, Missouri,] to Bishop [Joseph] Rosati [in St. Louis, Missouri], December 19, 1833. St. Louis, MO: Archives of the Archdiocese of St. Louis, n.p.

Letter from John Boullier to Bishop Rosati, August 5, 1835. St. Louis, MO: Archives of the Archdiocese of St. Louis, n.p.

Letter from John Boullier to Bishop Rosati, January 17, 1837. St. Louis, MO: Archives of the Archdiocese of St. Louis, n.p.

Livre de Dispenses des Marriages 1840. St. Joachim Church, Old Mines, MO: n.p.

March, David D. *The History of Missouri*. 4 vols. New York, NY: Lewis Historical, 1967.

Marriage Records of the Church of St. Joachim, Old Mines: Volume I: September 2, 1851–September 7, 1897. Old Mines, MO: n.p.

Miles, John T. "Old Mines, Missouri: A Typical French Community in Washington County." In *History and Customs of Washington, Iron, St. Francois, and Ste. Genevieve Counties*. N.p., 1937.

Miller, Samuel J. "Peter Richard Kenrick Bishop and Archbishop of St. Louis 1806–1896." *Records of the American Catholic Historical Society of Philadelphia* 84:1–3 (1973) 3–163.

Mortuaires de 1836 a 1851; Liber Defunctorum Parochia S. Joachim Loci Veterium Minarum Inchoatus 16 September 1836. Old Mines, MO: n.p.

Notes: Lending Library of 1866, List of 196 Books of this Library, Names of Borrowers, Financial Account of Library 1866, List of Pew Renters of St. Joachim 1866, Rosary Society of 1833, Church Account of 1882, Contributors for Support of Pastor 1888, St. Joseph Society Account of 1889, First Communion Class of 1833, 1889. Old Mines, MO: St. Joachim Church, n.p.

Parish Census of 1890. St. Joachim Church, Old Mines, MO: n.p.

Payton, Crystal, ed. John Hogan, *On the Mission in Missouri 1857–1868, Fifty Year Ago: A Memoir*. Springfield, MO: Lens and Pen, 2009.

Payton, Leland, and Crystal Payton. *Mystery of the Irish Wilderness: Land and Legend of Father John Joseph Hogan's Lost Irish Colony in the Ozark Wilderness*. Springfield, MO: Lens and Pen, 2008.

Post, Truman A. "Peter Richard Kenrick, Appellant, Vs. George B Cole, Executor of Mary L. Lamarque, et. al., Respondents." In *Reports of Cases Argued and Determined in the Supreme Court of the State of Missouri*. St. Louis, MO: St. Louis Democrat Co. 61 (1975–6) 576–7.

———. "Peter Richard Kenrick, Defendant in Error, Vs. George B. Cole and Louis Bolduc, Plaintiffs in Error." In *Reports of Cases Argued and Determined in the Supreme Court of the State of Missouri*. St. Louis, MO: St. Louis Democrat Co. 46 (1878) 88-9, 191.

"Recapitulation of the Settlement of the Estate of Marie L. Lamarque." In *Washington County Index to the Probate Record Book: Book C*. Potosi, MO: Washington County Court House, n.p.

"Recapitulation of the Settlement of the Estate of Marie L. Lamarque by George B. Cole, July 12, 1876." File No. 563. Potosi, MO: Archives of the Probate and Magistrate Court of Washington County, n.p.

Register of Marriages 1836–1851. St. Joachim Church, Old Mines, MO: n.p.

Register of St. Joachim Church, Old Mines, Missouri, 1820–1827. St. Louis, MO: Archives of the Archdiocese of St. Louis, n.p.

Registre des Baptismes July 9, 1836–July 7, 1847. St. Joachim Church, Old Mines, MO: n.p.

Registre des Baptismes et Mariages de la Pariosse St. Joachim, Vieille Mine, September 20, 1827–July 9, 1836. Old Mines, MO: n.p.

Registres de Insinuations. Perrin Collection. St. Clair County, Illinois State Library: Cahokia Records, n.p.

Registrum Baptismorum of the Church of St. Joachim, Old Mines, January 19, 1908–July 10, 1921. Old Mines, MO: n.p.

Rothensteiner, John. *History of the Archdiocese of St. Louis.* St. Louis, MO: Blackwell Wielandy, 1928.

"St. James Catholic Church." https://stjamespotosi.org/our-parish/parish-history.

Ste. Genevieve Church Records: Baptisms and Marriages, Book A. Ste. Genevieve, MO: n.p.

————: *First Book of Burials.* Ste. Genevieve, MO: n.p.

————: *Marriages, Book B.* Ste. Genevieve, MO: n.p.

————: *Register of Marriages.* Ste. Genevieve, MO: n.p.

"Sale of Beauvais Estate." April 21, 1776. Ste. Genevieve, MO: Ste. Genevieve Court House Archives, n.p.

Sauer, Carl O. *The Geography of the Ozark Highland of Missouri.* The Geographical Society of Chicago Bulletin No. 7. Chicago, IL: University of Chicago Press, 1920.

Scharf, J[ohn]. Thomas. *History of St. Louis City and County from the Earliest Periods to the Present Day.* 2 vols. Philadelphia, PA: Louis H. Everts & Co., 1883.

Sullivan, Dan. "Irish in Missouri." http://dsullivanadaircountyr1.weebly.com/irish-immigration-in-missouri.html.

"Supreme Court of the State of Missouri at St. Louis: Peter R. Kenrick, Defendant in Error, Vs. George B. Cole and Louis Bolduc, Plaintiffs in Error: Statement of defendant in Error." Jefferson City, MO: Missouri Supreme Court Archives, n.p.

Tanguary, Cyprian. *Dictionnaire Genealogique de Familles Canadiennes depuis a la Foundation de la Colonie jusq'a Nos Jours.* 7 vols. Montreal, Canada: E. Senecal, 1871–1891.

"Tour of the Bolduc House." Ste. Genevieve, MO, July 23, 1975.

Transcribed Record of Marriages Kept in the Church of Ste. Genevieve. Ste Genevieve, MO: n.p.

Transcript from the Register of Births and Baptisms Kept in the Roman Catholic Church of Ste. Genevieve. Ste. Genevieve, MO: n.p.

"Transcript of Missouri Supreme Court Case: Peter Richard Kenrick, Defendant in Error, Vs. George B, Cole and Louis Bolduc, Plaintiffs in Error." Jefferson City, MO: Missouri Supreme Court Archives, n.p.

"Transcript of Missouri Supreme Court Case: Peter Richard Kenrick Vs. George B. Cole, Executor of Mary L. Lamarque, et al." Jefferson City, MO: Missouri Supreme Court Archives, n.p.

Villmer, Natalie. *250th Anniversary Historical Program-Pageant Book.* Flat River, MO: Hollard Printing Service, 1973.

Washington County Deed Record Books: Book A. Potosi, MO: Washington County Court House, n.p.

————: *Book B.* Potosi, MO: Washington County Court House, n.p.

————: *Book C.* Potosi, MO: Washington County Court House, n.p.

————: *Book D.* Potosi, MO: Washington County Court House, n.p.

————: *Book E.* Potosi, MO: Washington County Court House, n.p.

————: *Book F.* Potosi, MO: Washington County Court House, n.p.

————: *Book G.* Potosi, MO: Washington County Court House, n.p.

————: *Book H.* Potosi, MO: Washington County Court House, n.p.

————: *Book I.* Potosi, MO: Washington County Court House, n.p.

————: *Book J.* Potosi, MO: Washington County Court House, n.p.

————: *Book K.* Potosi, MO: Washington County Court House, n.p.

————: *Book L.* Potosi, MO: Washington County Court House, n.p.

————: *Book M.* Potosi, MO: Washington County Court House, n.p.

————: *Book N.* Potosi, MO: Washington County Court House, n.p.

————: *Book O.* Potosi, MO: Washington County Court House, n.p.

"Western Catholic Historical Notes." In *The American Catholic Historical Researches*, New Series 2:1 (January 1906) 92–5.

Whitman, Walt. "Pioneers! O Pioneers!" In *Leaves of Grass.* https://whitman archive.org/published/LG/1891/poems/99.

Recent Books by Mark G. Boyer
published by Wipf & Stock

Nature Spirituality: Praying with Wind, Water, Earth, Fire

A Spirituality of Ageing

Weekday Saints: Reflections on Their Scriptures

Human Wholeness: A Spirituality of Relationship

A Simple Systematic Mariology

Praying Your Way through Luke's Gospel and the Acts of the Apostles

An Abecedarian of Animal Spirit Guides: Spiritual Growth through Reflections on Creatures

Overcome with Paschal Joy: Chanting through Lent and Easter— Daily Reflections with Familiar Hymns

Taking Leave of Your Home: Moving in the Peace of Christ

An Abecedarian of Sacred Trees: Spiritual Growth through Reflections on Woody Plants

Divine Presence: Elements of Biblical Theophanies

Fruit of the Vine: A Biblical Spirituality of Wine

Names for Jesus: Reflections for Advent and Christmas

Talk to God and Listen to the Casual Reply: Experiencing the Spirituality of John Denver

Christ Our Passover Has Been Sacrificed: A Guide through Paschal Mystery Spirituality—Mystical Theology in The Roman Missal

Rosary Primer: The Prayers, The Mysteries, and the New Testament

From Contemplation to Action: The Spiritual Process of Divine Discernment Using Elijah and Elisha as Models

Love Addict

All Things Mary: Honoring the Mother of God—An Anthology of Marian Reflections

Shhh! The Sound of Sheer Silence: A Biblical Spirituality that Transforms

What is Born of the Spirit is Spirit: A Biblical Spirituality of Spirit

Very Short Reflections—for Advent and Christmas, Lent and Easter, Ordinary Time, and Saints—through the Liturgical Year

Living Parables: Today's Versions

My Life of Ministry, Writing, Teaching, and Traveling: The Autobiography of an Old Mines Missionary

300 Years of the French in Old Mines: A Narrative History of the Oldest Village in Missouri

Journey into God: Spiritual Reflections for Travelers

Monthly Entries for the Spiritual but not Religious through the Year: Texts, Reflections, Journal/Meditations, and Prayers for the Spiritual but not Religious

The Shelbydog Chronicles by Shelby Cole as Recorded by Mark G. Boyer: A Novel

www.ingramcontent.com/pod-product-compliance
Lightning Source LLC
Chambersburg PA
CBHW071107090426

42737CB00013B/2516